To Rachel~
So glad
have you at 2/2015
♡ you.

Faith Over Feelings

Elaine Kennelly
1 John 5:4-5

Faith Over Feelings
Learning to Know God and Trust Him
By Elaine Kennelly

Copyright 2015 Elaine M. Kennelly
All Rights Reserved. This book is protected under the copyright laws of
the United States of America. This book may not be copied or reprinted
for commercial gain or profit. No portion of this publication may be
reproduced, stored in a retrieval system, or transmitted in any form by any
means.

Cover Design: Laura Griffin

ISBN: 978-0-9864320-0-2

eISBN: 978-0-9864320-1-9

*This book is published in conjunction with the website
Something Sisters.com written by Elaine Kennelly*

Unless otherwise indicated, Scripture verses quoted are taken from the
New Living Translation (NLT) 1996. Tyndale House Publishers, Inc.
Other translations:
The Message (MSG) Nav Press Publishing Group
New International Version (NIV) Zondervan Publishers
Contemporary English Version (CEV) American Bible Society
GOD'S WORD Translation (GWT) Baker Publishing Group

Printed in the U.S.A.

Faith
Over
Feelings

Learning to Know God and Trust Him

Elaine Kennelly

*Therefore, since we have been made right in God's sight by **faith**, we have peace with God because of what Jesus Christ our Lord has done for us.*

*Because of our **faith**, Christ has brought us into this place of undeserved privilege where we now stand, and we confidently and joyfully look forward to sharing God's glory.*

Romans 5: 1-2

This book is dedicated to the
Lord Jesus Christ
and to
His followers worldwide.

Contents

Introduction

Everyone lives by faith. Did you ever question or worry about the sun rising the next day or gravity being reversed? Could 24 hours suddenly change to 12? Will Earth fall off its axis?

Do you purposefully say to yourself, "Heart, keep beating." Must you remind your stomach to process what you have just put into it, or do you tell your nose when to sneeze? Of course not, because we all live by faith.

There comes a time, however, when life's circumstances overtake us. Jesus calls these times "troubles." We would call them divorce, pain, sickness, death, bankruptcy, addictions, grief, heartache. This is when our faith allows us to live above our feelings. Faith over feelings is a choice, a lifestyle, a learned path to living in the strength of our faith in God. How much faith do you have? Or better said--how much faith do you want? You have the choice.

What Is Faith?

Let's use the definition God uses. *"Faith is the confidence that what we hope for will actually happen. It gives us assurance about things we cannot see." Hebrews 11:1* We cannot see gravity, but we have confidence it is working. We have assurance the sun will rise and set according to what God has created.

Hebrews 11:1 also applies to our spiritual beliefs, to the way we live, think, and relate to God. Some say they do not believe there is a God. Well, actually, there are two kinds of atheists -- the live ones who don't believe in God, and the dead ones who do.

So faith comes from hearing, that is, hearing the Good News about Christ. Romans 10:17

v

For in the Gospel the righteousness of God is revealed -- a righteousness that is by faith from first to last, just as it is written: "The righteous will live by faith." Romans 1:17 NIV

...keeping our eyes on Jesus, the champion who initiates and perfects our faith. Hebrews 12:2A

We live by faith, not by sight. 2 Corinthians 5:7 NIV

For in Christ, neither our most conscientious religion nor disregard of religion amounts to anything. What matters is something far more interior: Faith expressed in love. Galatians 5:5 MSG

When people work, their wages are not a gift, but something they have earned. But people are counted as righteous, not because of their work, but because of their faith in God who forgives sinners. Romans 4:4-5

So we are made right with God through faith and not by obeying the law. Romans 3:28

You love [Jesus] though you have never seen Him. Though you do not see him now, you trust Him and you rejoice with a glorious, inexpressible joy. The reward for trusting Him will be the salvation of your souls. 1 Peter 1:8-9

For every child of God defeats this evil world, and we achieve this victory through our faith. 1 John 5:4

Here are other definitions of Christian faith:

❖ Faith is a living, daring confidence in God's grace, so sure and certain that the believer would stake his life on it a thousand times. This knowledge of and confidence in God's grace makes people glad and bold and happy in dealing with God and with all creatures.

Martin Luther

❖ Faith is the deliberate confidence in the character of God whose ways you may not understand at the time.

Oswald Chambers

❖ Faith is seeing the invisible, knowing the unknowable; believing the unbelievable, so that you can achieve the impossible.

Stuart Briscoe

❖ Christian faith is acceptance of the promises and the work of Jesus Christ.

Milliard Erickson

❖ Saving faith is trust in Jesus Christ as a living person for forgiveness of sins and for eternal life with God.

Wayne Grudem

❖ Faith is resting in the Presence of God, even when circumstances are overwhelming. Faith is knowing and trusting that God, the Father, Son, and Holy Spirit is more than I will ever need.

Elaine Kennelly

What about Feelings?

Our world, our culture, our families, our lives, are fueled by feelings. Yes, God created us with emotions, but most feelings emoted are temporary. They aren't necessarily right or wrong -- they just are. They often change immediately after being spoken.

In fact, Clinical Psychologist Joseph Shannon, Ph.D. and other mental health professionals tell us there are really only five core feelings: anger, happiness, sadness, fear and disgust.

Here's what I think about feelings. First of all, there are more than five. Ask any woman for a vote on that!

But, feelings come and go; stress goes up and down; moodiness is everywhere; feelings are fickle; emotions can hurt deeply, temperaments can become volatile, and as our pastor repeatedly tells us, "Life is messy."

As followers of the Lord Jesus Christ, we need to understand that the Holy Spirit does speak to us within our emotions, and Jesus is a good example in John 11--weeping over the death of Lazarus.

However, it is also necessary to put our faith above our feelings. Faith in God, Father, Son and Holy Spirit, is the solid foundation of our lives. Life-decisions being made every day need to be based on God's words to us in Scripture, and the Holy Spirit working in our hearts and minds, not simply on how we might feel at any given moment.

Will we be perfect? Absolutely not! We are sinners saved by grace; that's what Christians are.

However, as we grow in that grace, as we grow in our knowledge of God, learn more about God's words to us, and allow the Holy Spirit to work within us, guess what? We will make better decisions. Our joy will increase, our confidence in God's promises will improve, our love will spread to more people, and our selfishness will decrease.

With faith in Jesus really taking hold of our lives, our anger, sadness, fear and disgust will dissipate, will disperse, will actually disintegrate. And what will fill that empty emotional space? The fullness of God will explode, exuding joy, love, mercy, grace, peace, goodness, trust, forgiveness, faith, thankfulness, perseverance, godliness, kindness, and self-control.

You see, when you finally empty yourself of all your negative emotional habits, you will have room for the fullness of God.

Don't let anyone capture you with empty philosophies and high-sounding nonsense that come from human thinking and from the spiritual powers of this world, rather than from Christ. For in Christ lives all the fullness of God in a human body. Colossians 2:8-9

How to Use This Book

Please use this book as a daily devotional. When you have finished it, start over again. Repetition helps recall. Nothing will draw you closer to Christ than time spent alone with Him.

Find your quiet time and quiet space every day and read at least one segment of this book. Don't read out of obligation. Read out of love for Jesus and your firm desire to grow a broader, deeper faith. Read the Bible verses out loud. Read slowly, not in a hurry, savoring the thought that God is talking to you AND listening to you. This is the most precious time of day for you -- when you are alone with Jesus. It is life-changing!

As you read the many passages chosen, the Holy Spirit will do His supernatural work within you. He will draw you to certain words, phrases and complete passages. There are three very important things to do:

MARK the words you are drawn to. Underline them, highlight them, write your thoughts in the margins. What is the Holy Spirit telling you? Reading God's words are different than reading any other words. God is speaking to you! Listen. *"Faith comes from hearing the message, and the message is heard through the word of Christ." Romans 10:17 NIV*

You might also enjoy writing some of these thoughts into a journal. Again, don't do it out of obligation. Let the Holy Spirit draw you into a deeper walk of faith over your feelings.

MEMORIZE the verse that the Holy Spirit is working within your mind and heart. I use 3 x 5 cards, writing down the words

God wants me to remember. Then I tape them where I will see them often -- like my bathroom mirror. It works.

MAKE IT YOURS as you go through your day. Repeat it, pray it, and thank God for giving you a special message. Remember, the King of Kings and Lord of Lords, the God of all creation is giving YOU His remarkable thoughts! What a gift!

Your faith will be deepened, I promise, by your embracing of Scripture. Journal your thoughts and Bible verses to help you.

Personalizing Scripture is a way of allowing your life to be totally intertwined with God. Example -- *The Lord has done great things for us, and we are filled with joy." Psalm 126: 3 NIV*

To personalize that message, say, "The Lord has done great things for me and I am filled with joy." Or better yet, "The Lord has done great things for _____, and I am filled with joy." Put your name in the blank. God loves to hear your name. After all, God reminds us that *"He has written your name on the palms of [His] hands." Isaiah 49:16*

My dear friends in Christ, if you are reading this, you are making a choice to grow closer to Jesus Christ. The best way for this to happen is for you to meet with Him, all alone, every day. Take your Bible with you, read, pray, and meet with God. Talk to him, pour out your heart to him, ask for His blessing, ask for Holy Spirit power. Then quietly listen to what He says to you. Write down the words and thoughts He gives to you at this time. Jesus, your Redeemer, is sharing Himself with you!

God speaks these words to you right now:

"I am teaching you today -- yes, you --so you will trust in the LORD." *Proverbs 22:19*

I will instruct you and teach you in the way you should go; I will counsel you with My loving eye on you. Psalm 32:8 NIV

"Because of Christ and our faith in Him, we can now come boldly and confidently into God's Presence." Ephesians 3:12

I encourage you to read this book many times, prayerfully, and with an open heart. Make a commitment to grow your faith now as you work through life's problems, receiving God's deep love for you, forgiveness and acceptance along the way, and expect to know God better as your faith deepens. Live expectantly! Daily be on an adventure with God. Daily live as His redeemed child.

God's Guarantee

Believing Grace,
Receiving Grace.
Fresh, daily Grace.
God's endless gift.
Forgiveness wrapped
Around me.... now!
A garment of salvation,
A robe of righteousness.
Fresh, generous, glorious Grace.
God's eternal gift.
ALL MINE!
Grace....
Always more than I will ever need.
God's favor, God's love,
By God decreed
Guaranteed.

Elaine Kennelly

Feelings

Sometimes I feel so empty, so tired, all alone.
My day feels lost. Needs aren't met. Weary to the bone.

Sometimes I feel so blue. Sadness deep inside me.
Don't know what to do, and no one here to guide me.

Sometimes I feel invisible -- life has passed me by.
I give, then give some more. Makes me want to cry.

I'm older now, yet there are those who daily need me;
My folks, my kids, but none emotionally feed me.

I have no peace, no joy, and have feelings of unrest.
Ha! Who said my golden years would be my best?

"I did," said Jesus as He listened to my thoughts.
"I have all you need. With My blood you were bought.

I give you countless blessings with My Grace.
I give you rest and joy, a smile on your face.

Your frantic pace of life has taken quite a toll,
Come to Me. I give blessed quiet for your soul."

Elaine Kennelly

Who Are You God?

**Sometimes, God, I feel so unsure, uncertain.
Do I really know you?   How will I recognize you?**

The heavens proclaim the glory of God. The skies display His craftsmanship. Day after day they continue to speak; night after night they make Him known. Psalm 19:1-2

For ever since the world was created, people have seen the earth and sky. Through everything God made, they can clearly see His invisible qualities -- His eternal power and divine nature. So they have no excuse for not knowing God. Romans 1:20

Dear friends, let us continue to love one another, for love comes from God. Anyone who loves is a child of God and knows God. But anyone who does not love does not know God, for God is love. 1 John 4:7-8

Only fools say in their hearts, "There is no God." They are corrupt, and their actions are evil; not one of them does good! The Lord looks down from heaven on the entire human race; He looks to see if anyone is truly wise, if anyone seeks God.
Psalm 14:1-2

"Be still, and know that I am God! I will be honored by every nation. I will be honored throughout the world."   Psalm 46:10

That is what the Scriptures mean when they say, "No eye has seen, no ear has heard, and no mind has imagined what God has prepared for those who love Him." But it was to us that God revealed these things by His Spirit. For His Spirit searches out everything and shows us God's deep secrets. 1 Cor. 2:9-10

Talking with God

Hello God, I know within my heart that You exist, that You are, and I am seeking You today. Help me to see You in all of the beauty around me: a single flower, a sky filled with clouds, sand on the beach, trees of all kinds, mountains, rain. Help me to see Your magnitude and Your generosity in providing colors, shapes, stars by the millions, and galaxies yet undiscovered. You are the Creator over all creation! You are Love to every human being.

Let me see You as love in people around me. Help me to be aware of love and eagerly look for it. But more important, Father, let me BE love to everyone I meet. Put someone in my path who needs Love, for You are Love. I will merely be the vessel used to give You away. What a privilege! Thank You for loving me first, even when I was a fool.

"Praise be to the God and Father of our Lord Jesus Christ, who has blessed us in the heavenly realms with every spiritual blessing in Christ. For [God] chose us in Him before the creation of the world to be holy and blameless in His sight." (Ephesians 1: 3-4)

Thank You for choosing me, O Holy God! Help me to prioritize my time to spend with You, for only then will I truly get to know You. My heart is filled with praise and glory to God! Amen

What will I choose to do in order to know God better?

What do I want to memorize today?

2

Who Are You Jesus?

Is this a stupid question? Should I feel embarrassed to even bring this up? The fact is -- I want to know You better. I desire a stronger relationship with You. Teach me, Jesus, about Yourself.

Mary asked the angel, "But how can this happen? I am a virgin." The angel replied, "The Holy Spirit will come upon you, and the power of the Most High will overshadow you. So the baby to be born will be called the Son of God.....and you will name Him Jesus." Luke 1:34-35 and 31B

"But what about you?" [Jesus] asked. "Who do you say I am?" Simon Peter answered, "You are the Messiah, the Son of the Living God." Matthew 16:15-16 NIV

For, there is one God and one Mediator who can reconcile God and humanity -- the man Christ Jesus. He gave His life to purchase freedom for everyone. 1 Timothy 2:5-6

For God called you to do good, even if it means suffering, just as Christ suffered for you. He is your example, and you must follow in His steps. 1 Peter 2:21

For in Christ lives all the fullness of God in a human body. Colossians 2:9

You must have the same attitude that Christ Jesus had. Though He was God, He did not think of equality with God as something to cling to. Instead, He gave up His divine privileges; He took the humble position of a slave and was born as a human being. When He appeared in human form, He humbled Himself in obedience to God and died a criminal's death on a cross. Philippians 2:5-8

Talking to God

Oh, Jesus, I come in prayer to You knowing full well You are the Son of God. You are the Creator of the world. You are my precious Savior, who was obedient to His Father and came into the world knowing He would die the bitter death of crucifixion in my place. I should have hung on the cross, but YOU took my place. You suffered the scourging. You embraced the humiliation and shame. You took the guilt of every person's sin, and the Father turned His back on You, His only Son, for just a moment.

There was no other way. There was no other plan except for You, dearest Jesus, to become sin in order to save every sinner, of whom I am the worst. What love, incomprehensible! What pure sacrifice! What a gift to ALL.! When you look at me, sweet Jesus, I am clean, washed in the blood of the Lamb. You see Your perfect child....I am holy and blameless as I stand before You without a single fault.

My faith in You, O Holy Son of God, is not performance-based. It is faith-based! I could never do enough good works to earn my salvation, and I could never do enough evil deeds to be turned away from salvation. Praise God that redemption is a gift to be received and believed. I pray and rest forever in the name of the Lamb, the Son of God, the Savior, Jesus, my Lord. Amen

Do you know, without any hesitation or doubt that you are forgiven through the death and resurrection of Jesus? _____

If not, read this prayer again and tell Jesus you believe in Him. Confess your sin and tell Him you believe that He died to save you from all sins, and you believe He has reconciled you into a relationship with God. Thank Him! Join with other believers to grow in the faith you have received.

Who Is the Holy Spirit?

I know pretty much about the Father and Jesus, but I feel confused about the Holy Spirit. What exactly does the Holy Spirit do?

And everyone present was filled with the Holy Spirit and began speaking in other languages, as the Holy Spirit gave them this ability. Acts 2:4

[Jesus said] "But you will receive power when the Holy Spirit comes upon you. And you will be my witnesses"....Acts 1:8

God Himself showed that His message was true by working all kinds of powerful miracles and wonders. He also gave His Holy Spirit to anyone He chose. Hebrews 2:4   CEV

But the Spirit makes us sure God will accept us because of our faith in Christ. Galatians 5:5   CEV

The Holy Spirit produces this kind of fruit in our lives: love, joy, peace, patience, kindness, goodness, faithfulness, gentleness, and self-control. There is no law against these things!   Gal. 5:22-23

Since we are living by the Spirit, let us follow the Spirit's leading in every part of our lives. Galatians 5:25

It is God who enables us, along with you, to stand firm for Christ. He has commissioned us, and He has identified us as His own by placing the Holy Spirit in our hearts as the first installment that guarantees everything He has promised us. 2 Corinthians 1:21-22

My friends, the Lord loves you, and it is only natural for us to thank God for you. God chose you to be the first ones to be saved. His Spirit made you holy, and you put your faith in the truth. 2 Thessalonians 2:13   CEV

5

Talking to God

Holy Spirit of God, I am awed by what You do for me, and it is a great gift. You give me faith, and You give me a new life in Christ. As it says in Scripture, "For all who are led by the Spirit of God are children of God." (Romans 8:14) Oh, how I love being Your child! I am a daughter/son of the Almighty God, a daughter/son of the King! And with that comes privilege -- I am an heir, written into the will. I have eternal life waiting for me when I die, and guess what? I am going to die, but I need not fear death, for I KNOW, without a doubt that I am just one step away from the Presence of God! In fact, I am already enjoying the benefits of Heaven -- my sins are forgiven, my focus is on God and, I worship Him along with all of the Heavenly Host. Wow!

And then I receive another fabulous gift. It says in Isaiah 44:3 that "God will pour out His Spirit on my descendants, and His blessings will be on my children." (Author paraphrase.) Pour out Your precious blessings on my children and grandchildren. Oh, how I appreciate that, Lord. Your goodness is flowing from Your heart to my children. Thank You! Thank You! Thank You!

Holy Spirit, You also live in me. I am not my own, and I bow in surrender to You my body, mind, and soul. I am forever Yours as I pray to You and give my life to You. In Jesus' name. Amen

> Those in whom the Spirit comes to live are God's new Temple. They are, individually and corporately, places where heaven and earth meet.
> N. T. Wright
> *Simply Christian: Why Christianity Makes Sense*

Assurance

Doubt sometimes creeps into my thoughts, especially when I am alone. If I believe in Jesus, are ALL my sins forgiven? Will I go to Heaven when I die?

[Jesus said] "I tell you the truth, those who listen to my message and believe in God who sent Me have eternal life. They will never be condemned for their sins, but they have already passed from death into life." John 5:24

There is salvation in no one else! God has given no other name [than Jesus] under heaven by which we must be saved. Act 4:12

For God's will was for us to be made holy by the sacrifice of the body of Jesus Christ, once for all time. Hebrews 10:10

For God loved the world so much that He gave His one and only Son, so that everyone who believes in Him will not perish but have eternal life. John 3:16

Jesus said, "Yes, I am the gate. Those who come in through Me will be saved." John 10:9

God saved you by His grace when you believed. And you can't take credit for this; it is a gift from God. Salvation is not a reward for the good things we have done, so none of us can boast about it. Ephesians 2:8-9

Jesus told her, "I am the resurrection and the life. Anyone who believes in Me will live, even after dying. Everyone who lives in Me and believes in Me will never die. Do you believe this, _____?" John 11:25 (Put your name in the blank.)

Talking with God

Dear Sweet Jesus, my heart overflows with love for You, and I have a deep sense of gratitude for Your gift of Grace. You left Heaven for me and took on a human body for me. You were obedient to your Father even if His plan was crucifixion in order to die on my behalf. You had the power to come off that cross, but because of Your love and obedience, You stayed, suffered, and died for me. You took my place and paid the price by redeeming me from an eternity in hell. I repent of every sin that put you there, and I thank you for loving me so much! I am forgiven, once and for all, and as proof, God, Your Father raised You to life! Now I am free from the bondage of sin, and I know, without a doubt, that when I die, I will spend eternity in Heaven with You.

Jesus, allow me to share this precious gift with others. Give me a faith and a boldness to tell others about You and share with them the miracle of my salvation. In the name of my Savior, Jesus, I pray. Amen

Which Bible verse would be your favorite to personalize?
Write it here, so you can read it often.

This is the heart and soul of your faith. Do you believe this? Are you now assured of your Heavenly future? Tell God and write it here.

Worry

You already know this about me, God, but I worry about everything: job, health, kids, money. I need more faith, more trust. Help!

Trust in the LORD with all your heart; do not depend on your own understanding. Seek His will in all you do, and He will show you which path to take. Proverbs 3:5-6

Don't worry about anything; instead, pray about everything. Tell God what you need, and thank Him for all He has done. Then you will experience God's peace, which exceeds anything we can understand. His peace will guard your hearts and minds as you live in Christ Jesus. Philippians 4:6-7

Give all your worries and cares to God, for He cares about you. 1 Peter 5:7

Those who listen to instruction will prosper; those who trust the Lord will be joyful. Proverbs 16:20

Many sorrows come to the wicked, but unfailing love surrounds those who trust the Lord. Psalm 32:10

But I am trusting you, O Lord, saying, "You are my God!" My future is in your hands. Psalm 31:14-15A

Jesus said, "Don't let your hearts be troubled. Trust in God and trust also in Me." John 14:1

I pray that God, the source of hope, will fill you completely with joy and peace because you trust in Him. Then you will overflow with confident hope through the power of the Holy Spirit. Romans 15:13

Talking with God

Heavenly Father, I confess to you my sin of worry and pride and lack of trust. I can do nothing on my own, but with You, God, ALL things are possible. Let me see the error of my thinking. Let me understand that YOU are my God, King of Kings, Lord of Lords! If you are for me, who can be against me? May the Holy Spirit strengthen my faith and strengthen my resolve to put complete trust in You, knowing you love me very much. And when you test my faith with problems and trials, may I come forth refined as gold. Take out the unbelief of my heart and put strength in my soul.

From this day forward, I will put my trust in You, and I will live in trust, for you are my strength and shield, and I am reminded again that Your Word is truth. You cannot lie, and You will never stop loving me. Your love is extravagant, more than I will ever comprehend. Your love never fails even though I may feel unloved. Show me Your love in all its might and power, for I think I do not trust You because I do not KNOW how deep, and wide, and strong Your love is. NOTHING is able to separate me from Your all-encompassing love. Oh, how I thank and praise you in the name of my loving, precious Jesus. Amen

How will you put your trust in God as you daily walk with Him?

What words were you drawn to in these verses? Underline them and write them here.

Spiritual Confusion

I am often confused about how I get faith. I want a relationship with Jesus. How do I get it?

For God saved us and called us to live a holy life. He did this, not because we deserved it, but because that was His plan from before the beginning of time -- to show us His Grace through Christ Jesus. 2 Timothy 1:9

For I am not ashamed of this Good News about Christ. It is the power of God at work, saving everyone who believes--the Jew first and also the Gentile. This Good News tells us how God makes us right in His sight. This is accomplished from start to finish by faith. Romans 1:16-17A

But to all who believed Him [Jesus] and accepted Him, He gave the right to become children of God. They are reborn -- not with a physical birth resulting from human passion or plan, but a birth that comes from God. John 1:12-13

God, Himself, has prepared us for this, and as a guarantee, He has given us His Holy Spirit. 2 Corinthians 5:5

I delight greatly in the LORD; my soul rejoices in my God. For He has clothed me with garments of salvation and arrayed me in a robe of His righteousness. Isaiah 61:10A   NIV

And now, just as you accepted Christ Jesus as your Lord, you must continue to follow Him. Let your roots grow down into Him and let your lives be built on Him. Then your faith will grow strong in the truth you were taught, and you will overflow with thankfulness. Colossians 2:6-7

Thank God for this gift too wonderful for words! 2 Cor. 9:25

Talking to God

Oh, God, my Holy God, thank you for loving me first, and I don't even deserve it. No, I don't deserve anything from you, except hell. I am a sinner, and then I go around thinking that I don't need anyone but myself. Oh, how wrong I am! I need a God who will forgive my rebellious past and change my arrogant heart. I confess my sins to you, Jesus, for You died on the cross for me to pay the extreme price of my sin.

I believe you, Jesus, that You are the Son of God and the Savior for every person, including me.

I believe you, Father, and receive your gift of GRACE -- God's Redemption at Christ's Expense.

I believe that faith in Jesus is all I need, and no matter how much dirt is in my past or how much good I will ever do in the future, I can never be disowned, nor can I ever earn my way into the family of God. I am Your child through Christ alone.

In fact, some day, YOU will come and take me home to Heaven to be with you forever. That promise will never change because You never change, dear Jesus. I give my life, my heart and mind, my soul, and my future to You as I pray in my Savior's name. Amen.

"I am the way, the truth, and the life. No one can come to the Father except through me."

Jesus
John 14:6

Praise

Today is a happy day, Lord! I feel blessed, and I want to praise you for all you have done for me!

Sing to the LORD; praise His name. Each day proclaim the good news that He saves. Psalm 96:2

Blessed are those who have learned to acclaim you, who walk in the light of your presence, LORD. They rejoice in your name all day long; they celebrate your righteousness. Ps. 89:15-16 NIV

Let them praise the LORD for His great love and for the wonderful things He has done for them. Psalm 107:8

Therefore, let us offer through Jesus a continual sacrifice of praise to God, proclaiming our allegiance to His name. Hebrews 13:15

I will praise you, LORD, with all my heart; I will tell of all the marvelous things you have done. I will be filled with joy because of You. Psalm 9:1-2A

Satisfy us each morning with your unfailing love, so we may sing for joy to the end of our lives. Psalm 90:14

I will praise You, Lord, among the nations; I will sing of You among the peoples. For great is Your love, reaching to the heavens; Your faithfulness reaches to the skies. Be exalted, O God, above the heavens; let Your glory be over all the earth. Psalm 57:9-11 NIV

It is good to give thanks to the LORD, to sing praises to the Most High. It is good to proclaim Your unfailing love in the morning, Your faithfulness in the evening. Psalm 92:1-2

Talking to God

I feel honored that I can come to you, O Lord, with praise on my lips and happiness in my heart. I don't feel like this every day, so I am wanting You to know that I do love You, and I do appreciate all that You do for me even if I forget to tell you! My life has changed since I became a believer in Jesus Christ. No, not every day is wonderful, but I do know deep down in my soul that I have some joy and some happiness. I still struggle with issues in my life, but Your love, O God, has given me joy and hope and a reason to smile more often. I like that.

My faith in You and Your gift of salvation has given me hope that each day I will draw closer to you, and You will draw closer to me. When that happens, then joy becomes more evident. I feel happier. I am calmer. I want to praise You more and love You more and thank You more. It seems thankfulness brings me joy!

May each day find praise on my lips and thanks on my mind and happiness in my heart to You forever and ever. Amen

---

It's not that praise is a sort of magical incantation that makes us strong in faith and maneuvers God into doing what we want. Rather, through praise, we focus on God....and praise in turn increases our confidence in Him.

Ruth Myers
31 Days of Praise

Fear

Fear often grips me Lord. What can I cling to for strength? I want to change. Please help me.

I prayed to the LORD, and He answered me. He freed me from all my fears. Psalm 34:4

The eyes of the LORD search the whole earth in order to strengthen those whose hearts are fully committed to Him. 2 Chronicles 16:9A

But the Lord is faithful; He will strengthen you and guard you from the evil one. 2 Thessalonian. 3:3

Don't be afraid, for I am with you. Don't be discouraged, for I am your God. I will strengthen you and help you. I will hold you up with my victorious right hand. Isaiah 41:10

Such love has no fear, because perfect love expels all fear. If we are afraid, it is for fear of punishment, and this shows that we have not fully experienced His perfect love. 1 John 4:18

And my God will meet all your needs according to His glorious riches in Christ Jesus. Philippians 4:19   NIV

The LORD is for me so I will have no fear. What can mere people do to me? Psalm 118:6

The LORD is my light and my salvation -- so why should I be afraid? The LORD is my fortress, protecting me from danger, so why should I tremble?   Psalm 27:1

God is our refuge and strength, always ready to help in times of trouble. So we will not fear when earthquakes come and the mountains crumble into the sea.   Psalm 46:1-2

Talking to God

Oh, God You are my God, and I give You all my fears, my dismay, my anxieties, my distress, my phobias, my uneasiness and even the panic that sometimes sets in. I bring them all and lay them at the foot of the cross for Your forgiveness.

My sinful nature is all too willing to give in to fear. How foolish, for many of my fears never even come to pass. Help me to change through the power of the Holy Spirit. Strengthen my faith to depend and to trust You for everything, even if I cannot understand everything. Remind me, Father, that I am more than a conqueror through our Lord, Jesus Christ, who loves me. Remind me that nothing can separate me from Your love. Remind me that Your love has the power to "cast out" my fears. Wrap Your hedge of protection around me. I trust in You!

Change my negative thinking that I might be transformed into the likeness of You, Jesus. Give me Your peace and Your steadfast Spirit so that I will live a life of stillness and surrender with a calm in my soul. For me, faith is a calm in my soul, and I desire a deeper faith, O God. Bless me with Your gift of peace, which surpasses all understanding, as I give my heart to You. Amen

What is your greatest fear?

What fears of yours have never came to pass?

Do you want to change from being fearful? _____How will God help you to accomplish that? Ask Him and write down what He says to you.

Arrogance/Pride

God, you know what? I don't like arrogant people, and today I was one! How do I grow in humility?

God's Message: "Don't let the wise brag of their wisdom. Don't let heroes brag of their exploits. Don't let the rich brag of their riches. If you brag, brag of this and this only: that you understand and know Me. I'm God, and I act in loyal love. I do what's right and set things right and fair, and delight in those who do the same things. These are My trademarks." God's Decree.
Jeremiah 9:23-24   MSG

Do you think the Scriptures have no meaning? They say that God is passionate that the spirit He has placed within us should be faithful to Him. And He gives grace generously. As the Scriptures say, "God opposes the proud but gives grace to the humble."
James 4:5-6

So humble yourselves under the mighty power of God, and at the right time He will lift you up in honor. 1 Peter 5:6

Pride leads to conflict; those who take advice are wise. Proverbs 13:10

Haughtiness goes before destruction; humility precedes honor.
Proverbs 18:12

Love the LORD, all you godly ones! For the LORD protects those who are loyal to Him, but He harshly punishes the arrogant.
Psalm 31:23

Pride ends in humiliation, while humility brings honor.
Proverbs 29:23

Talking with God

Dear Heavenly Father, I come to You with head bowed low. Today, I have been arrogant and full of pride. I have lifted myself up and put others down. I am truly sorry and bring my selfishness to Your throne of Grace. Paul, the greatest missionary who ever lived, wrote about himself in a letter to Timothy, his student, "This is a trustworthy saying, and everyone should accept it: Christ Jesus came into the world to save sinners: -- and I am the worst of them all." (I Tim.1:15)

It will take Your supernatural power to change my way of thinking and my way of acting towards others. But, I am pouring out my heart and asking for Your Holy Spirit power to change me. Thank you, Father, for nailing my arrogance to the cross. Now I understand what a gift it is to be forgiven! We can stand before our Heavenly Father in perfect peace knowing our salvation is complete in Christ Jesus. I am a sinner saved by Grace. God loves me extravagantly! His love for me never fails and never ends!

And tomorrow, Lord, give me a spirit of humility and graciousness towards others. Let me think of others first before I think of myself. Help me to do this with my spouse, my children, my co-workers, and all whom You put in my path. I want others to see Jesus shining through me! I know you will honor this prayer as I pour out my feelings to You in the name of my forgiving Savior Jesus Christ. Amen

> As for me, may I never boast about anything
> except the cross of our Lord Jesus Christ.
> Paul of Tarsus
> Galatians 6:14

Joyfulness

Happiness is fickle. Joy is deep and endures even through tough times. I want more joy in my life.

Because You are my Helper, I sing for joy in the shadow of your wings. Psalm 63:7

You love justice and hate evil. Therefore God, your God, has anointed you, pouring out the oil of joy on you more than on anyone else. Ps. 45:7

Dear brothers and sisters, when troubles of any kind come our way, consider it an opportunity for great joy. James 1:2

Don't be dejected and sad, for the joy of the LORD is your strength! Nehemiah 8:10B

I told [My disciples] many things while I was with them in this world so they would be filled with My joy." John 17:13

"Oh, what joy for those whose disobedience is forgiven, whose sins are put out of sight. Yes, what joy for those whose record the LORD has cleared of sin." Romans 4: 7-8

"When you obey my commandments, you remain in My love, just as I obey my Father's commandments and remain in His love. I have told you these things so that you will be filled with My joy. Yes, your joy will overflow! This is My commandment: Love each other in the same way I have loved you." John 15:12-13

Weeping may last through the night, but joy comes with the morning. Psalm 30: 5B

Talking with God

Good Morning, Lord. today help me to radiate joy with a smile on my face. After all, Your joy is a blessing to me, and I desire for You, dear Father, to anoint me with the oil of joy. Fill my heart and mind with all of Your goodness, kindness, love, peace and joy, and then, let me give these gifts to others around me. My spouse needs Your joy--may I be the giver. My children need Your goodness--may I be the giver. Let me be your Joy-Giver today, Oh Lord.

When your faithful servant, Nehemiah, was attacked and besieged by troubles, he said, "The joy of the Lord is my strength." May that be my prayer today. When troubles come, and they will, let me look to You for answers and the strength to overcome. Please allow Your Joy to help me be strong when I need to be strong. You work in so many wonderful ways. Please work through me to give out Your joyful blessings. My desire is to be a joy-giver for Jesus Christ. I know that with Your power and Your Spirit filling me with joy, my mission will be accomplished, and for that I thank and praise You forever. In the joyful name of Jesus, I lift up my prayer to you. Amen

---

Lord God, You ask me to give thanks in all things today -- because You know that the feeling of joy begins in the action of thanksgiving. Today, cause me to do Your will, not mine and let me release my desire to protect my joy at all costs. Today, open my hand to joy in surrendered obedience.

Ann Voskamp
One Thousand Gifts

Prayer

I feel stuck when I want to pray to God. I know prayer is talking to God, but I need guidance.

[Jesus said] "Our Father which art in heaven, Hallowed be thy name. Thy kingdom come. Thy will be done on earth, as it is in heaven. Give us this day our daily bread. And forgive us our debts, as we forgive our debtors. And lead us not into temptation, but deliver us from evil; For thine is the kingdom, and the power, and the glory, forever. Amen.   Matthew 6:9-13 KJV

[Jesus said] "Here's what I want you to do: Find a quiet, secluded place so you won't be tempted to role-play before God. Just be there as simply and honestly as you can manage. The focus will shift from you to God, and you will begin to sense His grace. Matthew 6:6   MSG

Listen to my voice in the morning, LORD. Each morning I bring my requests to You and wait expectantly. Psalms 5:3

Look at this: look who got picked by God! He listens the split second I call to Him. Complain if you must, but don't lash out. Keep your mouth shut and let your heart do the talking.
Psalm 4:3-4   MSG

Give me happiness, O Lord, for I give myself to You. O Lord, You are so good, so ready to forgive, so full of unfailing love for all who ask for your help. Psalm 86:4-5

Bend down, O LORD, and hear my prayer; answer me, for I need your help. Protect me, for I am devoted to You. Save me, for I serve You and trust You. You are my God. Psalm 86:1-2

Give thanks to the LORD, for He is good! Psalm 107:1A

Talking to God

Dear God, I am going to talk to You even if I am unsure of what to say and how to say it. I will think of prayer as talking on the phone with you or even writing a letter to you. I don't want to just text You a message -- that would be too short. I have a lot to say.

First of all, I finally realized that I am a sinner and need forgiveness. I have repented and received Jesus into my heart and life. I want You to know I love you, and I love what Jesus did for me by dying on the cross. I am Your child for real. I belong to the family of God. I never before felt I belonged anywhere.

I enjoy going to church although I'm not there every Sunday. I need to hear about Jesus and learn more about Him and His plan for me. I have some hang-ups that I don't know how to deal with, so please help me with that. Keep my anger from flaring up suddenly even with people I love -- especially with people I love.

Help me God, to be kind and loving to my family and friends. I want to forgive people who have hurt me, but I can't do it without You. I don't know how to do it. Bring some Christian person into my life to help me figure this out. I have started reading the Bible in the book called John. I never knew about all the miracles, and now I am a miracle, too! You know, this wasn't as hard as I thought it would be. I'm done. Amen

---

Prayer is not all speaking. It is listening to what God is sharing with you.

Elaine Kennelly

God's Love/Our Love

Feeling God's love and knowing God's love are two different things. Sometimes we just have to know for sure He loves us, even though we don't feel it.

And I am convinced that nothing can ever separate us from God's love. Neither death nor life, neither angels nor demons, neither our fears for today nor our worries about tomorrow -- not even the powers of hell can separate us from God's love. No power in the sky above or in the earth below -- indeed, nothing in all creation will ever be able to separate us from the love of God that is revealed in Christ Jesus our Lord. Romans 8:38-39

See how very much our Father loves us, for He calls us His children, and that is what we are! 1 John 3:1A

[Jesus said] "So now I am giving you a new commandment: Love each other. Just as I have loved you, you should love each other. Your love for one another will prove to the world that you are My disciples." John 13:34-35

Jesus replied, "You must love the LORD your God with all your heart, all your soul, and all your mind. This is the first and greatest commandment. A second is equally important: Love your neighbor as yourself." Matthew 22:37-39

For the LORD your God is living among you. He is a mighty Savior. He will take delight in you with gladness. With His love, He will calm all your fears. He will rejoice over you with joyful songs. Zephaniah 3:17

Love is patient and kind. Love is not jealous or boastful or proud or rude. It does not demand its own way. 1 Corinthians 13: 4-5A

Talking to God

I am awed by Your love for me, Papa. You call me Your child even though I choose sin over You many times. You love me more than I can ever comprehend, plus Your love never fails. It never changes. It never stops. You loved me first, drawing me into a love relationship with You. These are Your words to me, "I have loved you with an everlasting love; therefore I have continued my faithfulness to you." (Jeremiah 31:3)

Just praying this prayer causes me to feel Your unconditional love for me Lord, and yet there have been times in my life when I doubted Your love, because I didn't feel loved. This is exactly where my faith must overcome my feelings. I KNOW You love me regardless of how I feel. That is my prayer --to love You knowing full well that You are God and God is Love. Your love carries me through the trials and tribulations of my life. YOU are always more than I will ever need!

Your love has taught me to love others, even when I don't feel like it. In fact, You command me to love others. Here is where I need Your power. Fill my mind with the desire and intention to love everyone around me. Fill my heart with Your love that flows through me to others. I cannot do it on my own, but with Your strength, I can do all things and love everyone You have put in my life. I pray this in the power of Jesus. Amen

Write about a time in your life that you knew God loved you even though you did not feel loved.

In which Bible verse did the Holy Spirit speak to you?

Weariness

I am so tired, Lord. Little by little I feel totally drained. I look after everybody, but who looks after me? I need spiritual strength to help me now.

Then Jesus said, "Come to me, all of you who are weary and carry heavy burdens, and I will give you rest. Take my yoke upon you. Let me teach you, because I am humble and gentle at heart, and you will find rest for your souls. For my yoke is easy to bear, and the burden I give you is light." Matthew 11:28-30

As soon as I pray, you answer me; You encourage me by giving me strength. Psalm 138:3

This is what the Sovereign LORD, the Holy One of Israel, says: "Only in returning to me and resting in Me will you be saved. In quietness and confidence is your strength. But you would have none of it." Isaiah 30:15

Whom have I in heaven but You? I desire You more than anything on earth. My health may fail, and my spirit may grow weak, but God remains the strength of my heart; He is mine forever. Psalm 73:25-26

For I can do everything through Christ, who gives me strength. Philippians 4:13

The eyes of the LORD search the whole earth in order to strengthen those whose hearts are fully committed to Him.
2 Chronicles 16:9A

But those who trust in the LORD will find new strength. They will soar high on wings like eagles. Isaiah 40:31A

Talking to God

Dear Jesus, I'm sure You also experienced weariness. You walked everywhere, and people were always after You for healing, for blessing, for teaching, for releasing demons. Then you had the difficult task of training twelve men who were totally clueless. You never even had the same bed to sleep in every night. Yes, I am sure you understand my weariness. That makes me feel closer to You. I know You understand.

Help me, precious Lord, to look to You for strength just as You looked to Your Father for strength. Angels were sent to minister to you. Please send angels to strengthen me! I need restoration from my spiritual deadness, and only Your Holy Spirit can renew my little faith. I open my heart and give Your Spirit free reign to change me, empower me, forgive me, and fill me up with the strength of God. May this be a precious gift to me each day.

Then I will "run and not grow weary. Then I will walk and not faint" as Isaiah predicts. Then I can take your yoke and partner with you as I live each day in Your Presence and in Your Strength. I feel better already, just knowing that I am committed to You, trusting You and walking with You on the path You have created for me. I praise and thank You for giving me Yourself -- now, I have everything! In the strong name of Jesus I pray. Amen

Come, oh come, with thy broken heart, weary and worn with care. Come and kneel at the open door, Jesus is waiting there.   Fanny Crosby

Fanny Crosby became blind as young child. She did not let that daunt her faith. She wrote over 8000 hymns in her lifetime, including my favorite, *Blessed Assurance*.

Troubles/Trials

Jesus, You said we would have troubles, but I am overwhelmed with trouble, pain, heartache. Help me! I am stretched to the limit of what I can bear.

[Jesus said] "I have told you all this so that you may have peace in Me. Here on earth you will have many trials and sorrows. But take heart, because I have overcome the world." John 16:33

Is anyone crying for help? God is listening, ready to rescue you. If your heart is broken, you'll find God right there; If you're kicked in the gut, he'll help you catch your breath. Disciples so often get into trouble; still, God is there every time. Psalm 34: 17-19 MSG

LORD, hear my prayer! Listen to my plea! Don't turn away from me in my time of distress. Bend down to listen, and answer me quickly when I call to you. Psalm 102:1-2

So be truly glad. There is wonderful joy ahead, even though you must endure many trials for a little while. These trials will show that your faith is genuine. It is being tested as fire tests and purifies gold -- though your faith is far more precious than mere gold. 1 Peter 1:6-7A

Dear brothers and sisters, when troubles of any kind come your way, consider it an opportunity for great joy. For you know that when your faith is tested, your endurance is fully developed, you will be perfect and complete, needing nothing. James 1: 2-4

A final word: Be strong in the Lord and in His mighty power. Put on all of God's armor so that you will be able to stand firm against all strategies of the devil. Ephesians 6:10-11

Talking to God

Yes, my heart is broken, and my spirit is crushed. I am facing problems that seem overwhelming to me. Why Lord? I am even angry with You at times, and I don't mind telling you so! Oh, You know my thoughts anyway, so I might as well tell You. Please, please help me to trust You in every situation even when I do not understand. Help me to trust that Your Holy Spirit is leading and guiding me and giving me strength to survive. Perhaps you are allowing these problems to come so that my faith will be strengthened, and I will come out as refined gold. For You are my Heavenly Father, and I know in my mind -- You love me. I know You will faithfully stand next to me through every problem. I know I will survive, because You have said that Your love never fails, and I believe You. It says in Scripture, "The faithful love of the LORD never ends!" Thank You. Thank You. Thank You.

I surrender all my troubles to You, Jesus, and I will try not to take them back, thinking that I can solve my own problems. I know I cannot get through this pain without You. You are my source of strength and peace. I thank You for allowing me to come boldly before the throne of grace to ask for Your help. In Jesus faithful name, I lay my requests before You. Amen

What trouble and pain have I surrendered to God?

Which Bible verses will especially help me? Write them here and memorize them.

Sovereignty of God

I feel clueless. I hear "Sovereignty of God" and I don't know what it means. What is it?

The LORD does whatever pleases Him throughout all heaven and earth, and on the seas and in their depths. Psalm 135:6

But once [God] has made His decision, who can change His mind? Whatever He wants to do, He does. So He will do to me whatever He has planned. He controls my destiny. Job 23:13-14

God's riches, wisdom, and knowledge are so deep that it is impossible to explain His decisions or to understand His ways. "Who knows how the Lord thinks? Who can become His adviser?" Who gave the Lord something which the Lord must pay back? Everything is from Him and by Him and for Him. Romans 11:33-36A GWT

Our God is in the heavens, and He does as He wishes. Ps.115:3

How great is our Lord! His power is absolute! His understanding is beyond comprehension! Psalm 147:5

....Who are you, a mere human being, to argue with God? Should the thing that was created say to the one who created it, "Why have you made me like this?" Romans 9:20

"Be still, and know that I am God! I will be honored by every nation. I will be honored throughout the world." Psalm 46:10

And yet, O LORD, You are our Father. We are the clay, and You are the potter. We all are formed by Your hand. Isaiah 64:8

Talking to God

Oh, God, I bow humbly before Your Sovereignty. You are more than I will ever be able to comprehend, and I am glad, because if I could understand Your motives, I would be equal to You. My puny mind is total insignificance compared to Your Greatness! I surrender my life to Your plan, to Your blessings, and to Your trials and testing of my faith. As Job said, "The LORD gave me what I had, and the LORD has taken it away. Praise the name of the LORD!" I want a heart like Job, dear Lord. I want to praise and thank You for the bad in my life as well as the good.

I surrender to You my health, my marriage or lack of marriage, my children, my grandchildren, my job, my career, my retirement account, my mind, my friends, even the day of my death. You are in control of everything including all the details of my life, and I leave my life in Your hands, knowing You love me and that I am Your child.

Please help me to remember that "All things work together for the good of those who love God and are called according to His purpose." But You may choose to never show me, Lord, what the "good" is or when it will appear. I simply know You are total Goodness. You love me, and I am Your child. I love you, too. Amen

---

In the aftermath of tragedy, to gather up the debris of our faith, we call God on the carpet and demand He explain Himself, and He had better have a good reason for doing what He did. But the truth is that God, being God, doesn't need to explain His actions to anyone.

Ronald Dunn
When Heaven Is Silent

Obedience

I feel frustrated! The very things I know God wants me to do -- I don't. I resist being obedient to God. I want to melt my rebellious streak.

Even though Jesus was God's Son, He learned obedience from the things He suffered. Hebrews 5:8

Don't just listen to God's word. You must do what it says. Otherwise, you are only fooling yourselves...but if you look carefully into the perfect law that sets you free, and if you do what it says and don't forget what you heard, then God will bless you for doing it. James 1:22 and 25

Work hard to show the results of your salvation, obeying God with deep reverence and fear. For God is working in you, giving you the desire and the power to do what pleases Him. Philippians 2:12B-13

[Jesus said] "If you love Me, show it by doing what I've told you. I will talk to the Father, and He'll provide you another Friend so that you will always have someone with you. This Friend is the Spirit of Truth." John 14:15-17A   MSG

My old self has been crucified with Christ. It is no longer I who live, but Christ lives in me. So I live in this earthly body by trusting in the Son of God, who loved me and gave Himself for me. Galatians 2: 20-21

We destroy every proud obstacle that keeps people from knowing God. We capture their rebellious thoughts and teach them to obey Christ. 2 Corinthians 10:5

Do you think all God wants are sacrifices -- empty rituals just for show? He wants you to listen to Him! 1 Samuel 15:22A   MSG

Talking to God

Father God, this is a hard prayer for me to pray. Obedience comes by giving up control over my life -- giving up, yielding, letting go, surrendering, and submitting everything to You and Your plan. You do not suggest obedience, You command obedience.

At the same time, You know we are but dust, and You provide a Helper and Advocate, Your Gracious Holy Spirit. May He pour out blessings upon my heart, my mind, and into the very center of my soul to fill me with His love, comfort, and strength. My neediness and Your power are a perfect match. My desire is to be an obedient follower of the Lord Jesus Christ!

When I stumble, forgive me Father. When I am weak, give me Your strength. When You test me, help me to "come forth as gold." As You reveal Yourself to me through obedience, may I respond with a loving attitude and simple obedience, not making excuses or rationalizing my behavior. Take away any rebellious thoughts, and in their place, give me Your sweet spirit of peace and submission. In the blessed name of Jesus, I pray. Amen .

All of God's revealed truths are sealed until they are opened to us through obedience...and it is not study that brings understanding to you, but obedience. Even the smallest bit of obedience opens heaven and the deepest truths of God immediately become yours. Yet God will never reveal more truth about Himself to you, until you have obeyed what you already know.

Oswald Chambers
My Utmost for His Highest

Anger

My anger is a concern, and my temper flares quickly. It creates problems in relationships, and I really don't like my angry self. I want to change.

Understand this, my dear brothers and sisters: you must all be quick to listen, slow to speak, and slow to get angry. Human anger does not produce the righteousness God desires. So get rid of all the filth and evil in your lives, and humbly accept the word God has planted in your hearts, for it has the power to save your souls. James 1:19-21.

And don't sin by letting anger control you. Don't let the sun go down while you are still angry, for anger gives a foothold to the devil. Ephesians 4:26-27

Get rid of all bitterness, rage, anger, harsh words, and slander, as well as all types of evil behavior. Instead, be kind to each other, tenderhearted, forgiving one another, just as God through Christ has forgiven you. Ephesians 4:31-32

What is causing the quarrels and fights among you? Don't they come from the evil desires that war within you? You want what you don't have, so you scheme and kill to get it. You are jealous of what others have, but you can't get it, so you fight and wage war to take it away from them. Yet you don't have what you want because you don't ask God for it. And even when you ask, you don't get it because your motives are all wrong -- you want only what will give you pleasure. James 4:1-3

Don't be quick to fly off the handle. Anger boomerangs. You can spot a fool by the lumps on his head. Ecclesiastes 7:9 MSG

Talking to God

Lord Jesus Christ, I come to you today with the realization that I am often an angry person, even when I don't show it. My mind is angry, and inside, I am miserable, lacking strength, and full of lust....I want it NOW is what I feel. I deserve it NOW is how I act. Sometimes I am even angry at you, God.

As long as I am pouring out my heart to You, God, let me be totally honest. I let little things "eat at me." I think them over and over. I live them over and over, and I let anger build in me until I "spill over", and then I don't like myself at all. I know this is not living the Godly life You have ordained for me.

Thank You for bringing me to faith in Jesus. I now understand how guilt can be pardoned and my sin forgiven. In Christ and through His death and resurrection, I am pardoned, forgiven, reconciled, and made whole in Him! Even You, Jesus, became angry at the money-changers doing business in Your house of worship. Let me have a righteous anger over injustice and cruelty in the world. Take the focus, sweet Jesus, off of myself, for my life does not revolve around me. I want my life to revolve around YOU.

Fill me with Your Sweet Spirit of love, and let me be thankful for what I have and for what I don't have. Let the disappointment and anger just melt away as I trust in You. For in You, I can do all things because You will strengthen me. In Jesus' name. Amen

Write down one area of anger that you desire to be "melted"?

Worship

I feel close to You God when I worship You. I want my worship to be intimate, to be reverent, filled with awe toward You--always remembering that when I worship, I am in the Presence of God.

And so, dear brothers and sisters, I plead with you to give your bodies to God because of all He has done for you. Let them be a living and holy sacrifice -- the kind He will find acceptable. This is truly the way to worship Him. Don't copy the behavior and customs of this world, but let God transform you into a new person by changing the way you think. Romans 12: 1-2A

With all my heart I will praise You, O Lord my God. I will give glory to Your name forever, for Your love for me is very great. You have rescued me from the depths of death. Psalm 86:12-13

Therefore, let us offer through Jesus a continual sacrifice of praise to God, proclaiming our allegiance to His name. And don't forget to do good and to share with those in need. These are the sacrifices that please God. Hebrews 13: 15-16

Come, let us worship and bow down. Let us kneel before the LORD our maker, for He is our God. We are the people He watches over, the flock under His care. If only you would listen to His voice today! Psalm 95: 6-7

[Jesus said] "But the time is coming -- indeed it's here now -- when true worshipers will worship the Father in spirit and in truth. The Father is looking for those who will worship Him that way. For God is Spirit, so those who worship Him must worship in spirit and in truth." John 4: 23-24

Honor the LORD for the glory of His name. Worship the LORD in the splendor of His Holiness. Psalm 29:2

Talking to God

Glorious God, I fall on my knees in worship and adoration of You. Give me power by Your Spirit to worship You in spirit and in truth, for Your ways are the desire of my heart. I long to praise You and thank You for being the Great God that You are -- the great I AM, my Portion, my Sufficiency.

You are everything to me, and You are ALL I will ever need!

I come humbly before you today with an attitude of worship in every aspect of my life. I worship with words and song, but I also worship You with my life, the way I live for You, and the way I give back to You in time, talent, and treasure. I worship You in love and obedience to Your words. I worship You in how I treat my body. I worship You in how I treat the loved ones in my family or total strangers on the street.

My desire is to worship, praise, thank, and adore You every day, not just on Sunday or holidays. My entire life is an act of worship, proclaiming Your majesty and power, Your love and forgiveness. "Holy, holy, holy is the Lord God Almighty, who was, and is, and is to come. You are worthy, our Lord and God, to receive glory and honor and power, for You created all things, and by Your will, they were created and have their being." (Revelation 4:8B and 11) In the glorious name of Jesus, I offer up this prayer. Amen

---

In the end, worship can never be a
performance...It's got
to be an overflowing of the heart.
Matt Redman

Happiness

Today I am happy, Lord! I have received Your forgiveness....I am healthy....my first child was born...I'm a Grandmother....I got the job...she loves me...I'm free from addictions...I love you, Jesus!

I delight greatly in the LORD; my soul rejoices in my God. For He has clothed me with garments of salvation and arrayed me in a robe of His righteousness...... Isaiah 61:10A NIV

The LORD is my strength and my shield; my heart trusts in Him, and He helps me. My heart leaps for joy, and with my song I praise Him. Psalm 28:7 NIV

You will experience all these blessings if you obey the LORD your God: your towns and your fields will be blessed. Your children and your crops will be blessed. The offspring of your herds and flocks will be blessed. Your fruit baskets and breadboards will be blessed. Wherever you go and whatever you do, you will be blessed. Deuteronomy 28:2-6

The godly walk with integrity; blessed are their children who follow them. Proverbs 20:7

Teach me Your decrees, O LORD; I will keep them to the end. Give me understanding and I will obey Your instructions; I will put them into practice with all my heart. Make me walk along the path of Your commands, for that is where my happiness is found. Psalm 119: 33-35

So let's not get tired of doing what is good. At just the right time we will reap a harvest of blessing if we don't give up. Galatians 6:9

Talking to God

It is with great joy in my heart that I come to You, O Father! I am blessed today by You, and I receive ALL that You desire to give to me today. Today is a happy day for me because _____ _____.

You are such a generous heavenly Father, faithful in so many ways. I see your faithfulness as I look back on my life. You were with me through every trial and every test. You provided exactly what I needed at the time. Oh, I didn't always agree with Your choices for me, but now I see that everything was for my good, even if you have not shared with me what the "good" is! I trust you, dear Jesus, and with that comes happiness and joy.

I pray for others I know who are facing problems today. You have said in Scripture, "When times are good, be happy; but when times are bad, consider: God has made the one as well as the other." (Ecclesiastes 7:14) I lift up to You these friends, co-workers, and family members: _____ _____.

I truly am happy in You, dear Jesus, and thank You for gifting me with faith and for sending Your Holy Spirit to comfort and counsel me. I am blessed. I am happy. I am thankful. Amen

---

Be happy with those who are happy
and weep with those who weep.
Romans 12:15

Feeling Close to Jesus

I have felt close to you in the past, dear Jesus, but today I feel like I am drifting away from You. Is it You or is it me? I want to be a loyal follower.

Come close to God, and God will come close to you. Wash your hands, you sinners; purify your hearts, for your loyalty is divided between God and the world. James 4:8

And now, just as you accepted Christ Jesus as your Lord, you must continue to follow Him. Let your roots grow down into Him, and let your lives be built on Him. Then your faith will grow strong in the truth you were taught, and you will overflow with thankfulness. Colossians 2:6-7

Seek God while He is here to be found, pray to Him while He's close at hand. Let the wicked abandon their way of life and the evil their way of thinking. Let them come back to God, who is merciful, come back to our God, who is lavish with forgiveness. Isaiah 55: 6-7   MSG

[Jesus said] "Remain in Me, and I will remain in you. For a branch cannot produce fruit if it is severed from the vine, and you cannot be fruitful unless you remain in Me. Yes, I am the vine; you are the branches. Those who remain in Me, and I in them, will produce much fruit. For apart from Me you can do nothing." John 15:4-5

For God says, "At just the right time, I heard you. On the day of salvation, I helped you." Indeed, the "right time" is now. Today is the day of salvation. 2 Corinthians 6:2

Remember what it says: "Today when you hear His voice, don't harden your hearts"...... Hebrews 3:15A

Talking to God

Somewhere in my memory, Jesus, there is a song that says, "I am running to You, Lord. I am running to You Lord." Yes! I AM running to You in my heart and in my mind. I picture You with arms open wide, waiting, just waiting for me to be enfolded in Your love, to be protected, as a refuge from myself.

I am the prodigal son/daughter returning home to the Father who forgives, redeems, and reconciles me to Himself. You never drift away from me, but I allow my sinful self to make poor choices, and I allow myself to be influenced by the world. Forgive me, Father, for I have sinned. Thank you that the blood of Jesus Christ cleanses me from all sin! I am forgiven.

Help me to grow a faith with deep roots in the Word of God. Empower me to stand firm in my faith, proclaim my faith, and grow in knowledge of the Lord Jesus Christ. I want to "remain in You and have You remain in me." I am Your child, dear Jesus, and I dedicate myself to You. In thankfulness and trust, I pray in my Savior's name. Amen

What worldly influences have been tugging at your heart?

How can you set up boundaries to keep you grounded in Jesus Christ? Have you asked for His help?

How much time every day do you spend reading God's Word?

Betrayal

I was betrayed by someone I trusted. I feel hurt, in fact, more than hurt. I feel lied to and used. I don't deserve this!

You will look in vain for those who tried to conquer you. Those who attack you will come to nothing. For I hold you by your right hand -- I, the LORD Your God. And I say to you, "Don't be afraid. I am here to help you." Isaiah 41:12-13

The wicked plot against the godly; they snarl at them in defiance. But the Lord just laughs, for He sees their day of judgment coming. Psalm 37:12-13

So be truly glad. There is wonderful joy ahead, even though you must endure many trials for a little while. These trials will show that your faith is genuine. It is being tested as fire tests and purifies gold -- though your faith is far more precious than mere gold. 1 Peter 1:6-7A

Stop being angry! Turn from rage! Do not lose your temper -- it only leads to harm. Psalm 37:8

But even as Jesus said this, a crowd approached, led by Judas, one of the twelve disciples. Judas walked over to Jesus to greet Him with a kiss. But Jesus said, "Judas, would you betray the Son of Man with a kiss?" Luke 22:47-48

Dear brothers and sisters, when troubles of any kind come your way, consider it an opportunity for great joy. For you know that when your faith is tested, your endurance has a chance to grow. James 1:2-4

Talking to God

Oh, dearest Jesus, You were perfect and never sinned, yet one of Your very own disciples, one of Your closest friends, betrayed You and had You arrested which led to Your death by crucifixion. I, too, feel used and betrayed, but it is nothing compared to You. I am humbled by just thinking about Your betrayal. Yes, I feel terribly hurt and even used, but I am going to choose forgiveness instead of anger and revenge.

Can I really forgive? Because now I feel angry and wanting to get even -- to hurt the one who betrayed me and hurt me. Right now, revenge seems right to me. Please, dear Jesus, work a miracle in me. Take away the anger, and in its place, give me a forgiving spirit. Help me to choose peace instead of pain. Your Spirit is called the Counselor -- counsel me through the forgiveness process. I am putting my trust in YOU! Then I will be whole again. Then I will live knowing I did the right thing, and in the long run, THAT will bring me joy. Lord, thank you for living such a great example of forgiveness for me. Didn't You say that when we pray, we should say, "Forgive us our trespasses as we forgive those who trespass against us?" Help me to do that, dearest Friend, in whose name I pray. Amen

---

Jesus was arrested in that garden,
Betrayed by a kiss prearranged.
How impossible for us to imagine such love.
It was Judas He called His friend.

Elaine Kennelly
Something Sisters 31 Day Devotional

Sorrow/Grief

I am deeply saddened by my loss. My sorrow is overwhelming. Is there anywhere in God's Word that will affirm my intense sorrowful feelings?

O LORD, God of my salvation, I cry out to you by day. I come to You at night. Now hear my prayer; listen to my cry. For my life is full of troubles, and death draws near. I am as good as dead, like a strong man with no strength left. They have left me among the dead, and I lie like a corpse in a grave. I am forgotten, cut off from Your care. You have thrown me into the lowest pit, into the darkest depths. Your anger weighs me down; with wave after wave You have engulfed me.

You have driven my friends away by making me repulsive to them. I am in a trap with no way to escape. My eyes are blinded by my tears. Each day I beg for Your help, O LORD; I lift my hands to You for mercy. Are Your wonderful deeds of any use to the dead? Do the dead rise up and praise You? Can those in the grave declare Your unfailing love? Can they proclaim Your faithfulness in the place of destruction? Can the darkness speak of Your wonderful deeds? Can anyone in the land of forgetfulness talk about Your righteousness?

O LORD, I cry out to You. I will keep on pleading day by day. O LORD, why do You reject me? Why do You turn Your face from me? I have been sick and close to death since my youth. I stand helpless and desperate before Your terrors. Your fierce anger has overwhelmed me. Your terrors have paralyzed me. They swirl around me like flood waters all day long. They have engulfed me completely. You have taken away my companions and loved ones. Darkness is my closest friend. Psalm 88:1-18 (In its entirety.)

Talking to God

I have prayed this prayer many times, Dear Papa, but I come once again into Your Presence with this request: take away the pain. Take away the sadness, the intense sorrow that plagues me day after day. Take away the guilt which Satan accuses me of, and unfortunately, I listen to. I know he is wrong, but I have not the strength to overcome his lies. Give me Your power, O Lord. THEN I will be able to see Your light and use Your strength. I need Your holy protection during this time of grief and sorrow and pain and loss. I need YOU.

Thank you for putting Psalm 88 in Scripture. There is no happy ending. There are no sappy verses that seem like a quick fix. You understand pain, don't You dear Jesus? Father, You know what it is to lose a Son. I can only imagine the intense sadness in Heaven when Jesus left to become a helpless baby in a poor family, born in a filthy stable, the target of an insane emperor. Sometimes nothing makes sense, does it?

Your loving Grace is the only thing that brings relief. It is so radical, so unreasonable -- YOU, the Holy God of all Creation, love ME so much that YOU gave up Your Son to die for ME, chief of all sinners. You redeem me and give eternity to me in Your Presence as a gift, absolutely free, with no strings attached.

GRACE -- God's Redemption At Christ's Expense -- that is love, and that gives me solace for my soul. Thank you. Amen

---

The Lord cares deeply when His loved ones die.
Psalm 116:15

44

Waiting on the Lord

Sometimes I feel like You ignore me God. Are You listening? Are You answering my prayers?

For since the world began, no ear has heard and no eye has seen a God like You, who works for those who wait for Him!
Isaiah 64:4

Wait patiently for the LORD. Be brave and courageous. Yes, wait patiently for the LORD.   Psalm 27:14

"Who can know the LORD'S thoughts? Who knows enough to teach Him?" But we understand these things, for we have the mind of Christ.   1 Corinthians 2:16

But you must not forget this one thing, dear friends; a day is like a thousand years to the Lord, and a thousand years is like a day.
2 Peter 3:8

I wait quietly before God, for my victory comes from Him.
Psalm 62:1

So, it is good to wait quietly for salvation comes from the Lord.
Lamentations 3:26

Listen to my voice in the morning, LORD. Each morning I bring my requests to you and wait expectantly. Psalm 5:3

If we already have something, we don't need to hope for it. But if we look forward to something we don't yet have, we must wait patiently and confidently.   Romans 8:24B-25

LORD, hear my prayer! Listen to my plea! Don't turn away from me in my time of distress. Bend down to listen and answer me quickly when I call to You.   Psalm 102:1-2

Talking to God

Dear Heavenly Father, I know clearly that You answer every prayer of mine. I know that! Yet there are times when I feel ignored. Help me to put my faith and knowledge ahead of my feelings which are fleeting and fickle. Help me, through the counsel of the Holy Spirit, to understand that unanswered prayer is really an oxymoron. You answer every prayer, and Your answers are yes, no, not now, perhaps, maybe, in My time, never, absolutely not, of course, right now, today, and WAIT.

Why is waiting so difficult for me? Lust....I want it now....whether it is another pair of shoes or more joy in my life. (Incidentally, dear Jesus, as You know, I do not need another pair of shoes. I am very greedy about "things", and I already have more shoes than I can ever wear out in my lifetime.) Help me to be generous to others who really NEED shoes!

Here is the bottom line: YOUR TIMING IS ALWAYS PERFECT! I pray for a heart of contentment and a heart that waits upon the Lord with praise and joy. I pray for a heart that accepts and yields to every answer, even when You say, "No." It is not the number of prayers that brings an answer. It is Your Sovereign Love for us that gives the answer. Help me to revel in Your decisions for me and my family. I love You very much, and I am thrilled to be Your special daughter/son. In Jesus' faithful name I pray. Amen

What have you prayed for that God said, "Wait"?

How do you react when God gives an answer of "No"?

Loneliness

So often, God, I feel all alone. Even when people are around, I feel no connection with others. Is there anyone who loves me or would miss me if I were dead? How can I connect with You?

You will seek Me and find Me, when you search for Me with all your heart. Jeremiah 29:13 NKJV

Even if my father and mother abandon me, the Lord will hold me close. Psalm 27:10

[Jesus said] "No, I will not abandon you as orphans -- I will come to you." John 14:18

But you ask God for help, and He gave you the victory. God is always on the alert, constantly on the lookout for people who are totally committed to Him. 2 Chronicles 16:9A MSG

[Jesus said] "For everyone who asks, receives. Everyone who seeks, finds. And to everyone who knocks, the door will be opened. Matthew 7:8

God places the lonely in families; He sets the prisoners free and gives them joy. But He makes the rebellious live in a sun-scorched land. Psalm 68:6

Don't worry about anything; instead, pray about everything. Tell God what you need, and thank Him for all He has done. Then you will experience God's peace which exceeds anything we can understand. Philippians 4:6-7A

The LORD your God will always be at your side, and He will never abandon you. Deuteronomy 31: 6B CEV

Talking to God

Dear God, I am lonely and often afraid. Many times I find it difficult to connect with people which makes me hesitant to try to meet people. It's a vicious cycle, and I do not know what to do. In fact, this is the first time I am really pouring out my feelings to you. I do have a Bible, and I am happy to read the Bible verses in this little book. They have been speaking to me.

You asked me to search for You, to ask, to seek, to receive. I have never tried to do that. No, I always thought I was self-sufficient, but as I get older, I realize I need You. I need Your love, care, and companionship. So I am seeking You in this prayer. I am searching for You through this little book about feelings. As a child, I did have faith and went to church, but I fell away, thinking that the church was only filled with hypocrites anyway. How foolish I have been. Forgive my stubbornness and self-pity.

I promise to find my Bible and start reading it. Lead me to the verses that will fill me with hope. Let me find You and Your love. Lead me, dear Jesus, and listen to this prayer. I am seeking You with all my heart. Amen

---

Orphans of God
Who here among us has not been broken?
Who here among us is without guilt or pain?
So oft abandoned by our transgressions.
If such a thing as Grace exists,
Then Grace was made for lives like this.
There are no strangers.
There are no outcasts.
There are no orphans of God.
So many fallen, but hallelujah,
There are no orphans of God.
Written by Joel Lindsey and Twila LaBar

Trust

Lord, why is it so difficult to trust You fully? If I loved You more, would I trust You more?

Blessed are those who trust in the LORD and have made the LORD their hope and confidence. Jeremiah 17:7

[Jesus said] "I have come as a light to shine in this dark world, so that all who put their trust in Me will no longer remain in the dark." John 12:46

Trust in the LORD always, for the LORD GOD is the eternal Rock. LORD, we show our trust in You by obeying Your laws; our heart's desire is to glorify Your name. Isaiah 26: 4 and 8

Greed causes fighting; trusting the LORD leads to prosperity. Those who trust their own insight are foolish. Proverbs 28:25-26

Trust God from the bottom of your heart; don't try to figure out everything on your own. Listen for God's voice in everything you do, everywhere you go; He's the one who will keep you on track. Don't assume that you know it all. Proverbs 3:5-6 MSG

Teach those who are rich in this world not to be proud and not to trust in their money, which is so unreliable. Their trust should be in God, who richly gives us all we need for our enjoyment. 1 Timothy 6:17

Lord Almighty, blessed is the one who trusts in You. Psalm 84:12

But I trust in You, LORD; I say, "You are my God." Psalm 31:14

Then Christ will make His home in your hearts as you trust in Him. Your roots will grow down into God's love and keep you strong. Ephesians 3:17

Talking to God

Yes, Glorious Father, You are my God! I have the Lord of all the galaxies as my Father, my Savior, my Counselor! The King of Kings is my Papa. You look upon me and call me Your child.

Then how is it that I would feel more trusting if Bill Gates was my father? Why do I ever have a lack of trust in You, the God who owns everything? Why is my trust so feeble?

I do not understand the darkness, and how much I need a Savior.
I do not understand surrendering my life to Your sovereignty.
I do not understand trusting You on the path You have me.
I do not understand Your unending, unfailing, eternal love for me.

There it is. I have finally confessed my innermost feelings to You, dear Jesus. All of my pretense is gone. My heart and mind are fully exposed. I am driven to the cross where the blood of Jesus Christ cleanses me from all sin. You are my only hope for salvation. Your love covers all of my sin.

I do desire Your complete forgiveness.
I do desire to know You better and trust You more.
I do desire to be a committed follower of the Lord Jesus Christ.
I do desire for my faith to grow deeper and stronger in You.
That is my prayer, in the forgiving name of Jesus, I trust. Amen

---

Though my natural tendency is to analyze and try to figure things out, trusting Jesus is a far better way to live. I've realized how very limited my understanding is.

Sarah Young
Jesus Calling

Today I Want to Rock for Jesus!

I am feeling on fire for Jesus! Today I want to stop being lukewarm in my faith and start living as a committed follower of the Lord Jesus Christ.

Because of Christ and our faith in Him, we can now come boldly and confidently into God's Presence.   Ephesians 3:12

Tell everyone about God's power. His majesty shines down on Israel; His strength is mighty in the heavens. God is awesome in His sanctuary. The God of Israel gives power and strength to His people. Praise be to God!   Psalm 68:34-35

I bow before Your holy Temple as I worship. I praise Your name for Your unfailing love and faithfulness; for Your promises are backed by all the honor of Your name. As soon as I pray, You answer me; You encourage me by giving me strength.
Psalm 138: 2-3

So let's *do* it -- full of belief, confident that we're presentable inside and out. Let's keep a firm grip on the promises that keep us going. He always keeps His word. Hebrews 10:22-23   MSG

Study this Book of Instruction continually. Meditate on it day and night so you will be sure to obey everything written in it. Only then will you prosper and succeed in all you do. This is my command -- be strong and courageous! Do not be afraid or discouraged. For the LORD your God is with you wherever you go. Joshua 1:8-9

For I fully expect and hope that I will never be ashamed, but that I will continue to be bold for Christ, as I have been in the past. And I trust that my life will bring honor to Christ, whether I live or die. Philippians 1:20

Talking to God

It is with great joy that I lift my heart to You, O Loving Father. Thank You for giving me the generous gift of Grace. I believe in Your Son, Jesus Christ, and I know I am redeemed. I am ransomed. My sin is atoned for through Christ's death on the cross and His resurrection. He has given me victory over sin, Satan, the pull of the world, and the love of myself.

I am Your child, and I surrender my life to Your plan for me. I am proud to be a follower of Jesus Christ. I ask for Your Holy Spirit power to charge my life with purpose. Give me a willing spirit to go where You desire and do what You have designed for me to do. After all, You have equipped me to accomplish all the good deeds which You planned in advance for me to do. I want to do them. In fact, I know I'm on an adventure with You!

It is delightful to put my present and my future in Your hands. I am Yours forever. I give myself fully to the work of the Lord, and I know, beyond a doubt, that I will not labor in vain. You have promised that Your word will never return to You void. I believe that and trust in You completely. Continue to guide and lead me, and may I forever live for Jesus Christ! In love and thankfulness I pour out my heart to You in the name of Jesus. Amen

What do you think the Lord is leading you to do?

What spiritual gifts do you think God has specifically given to you?

Where can you serve others inside or outside the church?

Word Pictures of Jesus

I have heard about "the Lamb." Is this Jesus? Are there other word pictures of Jesus that would help me to know Him better?

And God piled all our sins, everything we've done wrong, on Him, on [Jesus]. He was beaten, He was tortured, but He didn't say a word. Like a lamb taken to be slaughtered and like a sheep being sheared, He took it all in silence. Isaiah 53:6B-7 MSG

[Jesus said] "I am the good shepherd. I know my own sheep, and they know Me, just as My Father knows Me and I know the Father. So I sacrifice My life for the sheep." John 10:14-15

[Jesus said] "Yes, I am the gate. Those who come in through me will be saved. They will come and go freely and will find good pastures." John 10:9

Jesus spoke to the people once more and said, "I am the light of the world. If you follow Me, you won't have to walk in darkness, because you will have the light that leads to life." John 8:12

Jesus replied, "I am the bread of life. Whoever comes to Me will never be hungry again. Whoever comes to Me will never be thirsty." John 6:35

Jesus told her, "I am the resurrection and the life. Anyone who believes in Me will live, even after dying. Everyone who lives in Me and believes in Me will never ever die. Do you believe this, _____" John 11:25-26 (Put your name in the blank.)

Jesus told him, "I am the way, the truth, and the life. No one can come to the Father except through me." John 14:6

Talking to God

Jesus, Jesus, what You did for me is extraordinary! The sins of every person were laid upon You -- even future sins! No wonder these words were uttered on the cross, "My God, My God, why have you forsaken me?" Sin separates me from God, and the only way to be reconciled to the Father is through the Lamb of God. Your life and death paid the price for my sin. I am grateful beyond words. There is not a big enough thank you to recognize the enormity of Your gift of Grace. There is nothing, absolutely nothing that can separate me from Your unfailing love!

You are my Shepherd, dear Jesus, guiding me, restoring me, protecting me. You are the Light of the World, drawing me out of the darkness of sin. Thank You! Thank You! Thank You! You feed me the bread of knowledge through Your Word, and I am hungry daily. I love to feed on Scripture. I desire to be filled up with You. The bread of Your Spirit is what I need to live a life pleasing to You. Fill me up, Lord.

You, precious Savior, are my Eternal Life, and Resurrection will take place because of You. I will live with You forever in the never-ending light of Your love. My heart is about to burst with gratitude! What can I give to you, beloved Savior, but my heart, my mind, and my life. All is Yours, as I thank you forever. Amen

---

The fulfillment and fruitfulness Jesus offers is found only in friendship with Him. It is the essence of life in God's vineyard. Jesus is the true Vine. We are the branches, drawing nourishment from Him. Enjoying Him. He is our true Friend. There is no life without Him.

Wayne Jacobsen
In My Father's Vineyard

Judging Others

Churches make me feel very uncomfortable. I feel judged by the clothes I wear, the length of my hair, tattoos, or even my age. But here is what I really want to know: will God ever judge me?

For we must all stand before Christ to be judged. We will each receive whatever we deserve for the good or evil we have done in this earthly body. 2 Corinthians 5:10

Don't speak evil against each other, dear brothers and sisters. If you criticize and judge each other, then you are criticizing and judging God's law. But your job is to obey the law, not to judge whether it applies to you. God alone, who gave the law, is the Judge. He alone has the power to save or to destroy. So what right do you have to judge your neighbor? James 4:11-12

[Apostle Paul said] "I care very little if I am judged by you or by any human court; indeed, I do not even judge myself. My conscience is clear, but that does not make me innocent. It is the Lord who judges me. Therefore judge nothing before the appointed time; wait till the Lord comes. He will bring to light what is hidden in darkness and will expose the motives of the hearts. At that time each will receive his praise from God."
1 Corinthians 4:3-5   NIV

[Jesus said] "Do not judge others, and you will not be judged. Do not condemn others, or it will all come back against you. Forgive others, and you will be forgiven." Luke 6:37

I solemnly urge you in the presence of God and Christ Jesus, who will someday judge the living and the dead when He appears to set up His Kingdom. 2 Timothy 4:1

Talking to God

Father God, I have learned something important. For years, I have thought poorly about people who go to church because I thought church-goers were judgmental people, looking down on others. You know, hypocrites. Well, some of them are, but some are not. I guess I've learned I need to be less judgmental myself!

What I have also learned from Scripture is that You, Jesus, will judge all people sooner or later. I am reminded of sowing and reaping. "You will always harvest what you plant," the Bible says. Holy Spirit help me to plant love, goodness, kindness and truth.

Knowing the truth is good. Applying the truth to my life is where I need your help, Father. Teach me today and every day to love people, not judge them. Help me to be more generous in giving to others who are not as blessed as I am. I need Your Spirit of sharing and giving and doing all with a cheerful heart.

Here is something I am needing, O Lord: to be content to take second place, to allow others to be more important than me, to not always have life go my way. I don't want to be full of myself, but instead, to be full of You and Your love for others. With Your help, I know I can change! I am always grateful for Your help in making me a better Christian. Thank you, dear Jesus. Amen

---

But God told Samuel, "Looks aren't everything. Don't be impressed with His looks and stature. I've already eliminated him. God judges persons differently than humans do. Men and women look at the face; God looks into the heart."
1 Samuel 16:7   MSG

God's Plan for My Life

I feel very nervous. I don't know what God's plan is for my life. Now what?

The LORD says, "I will guide you along the best pathway for your life. I will advise you and watch over you. Psalm 32:8

[Jesus said] "My sheep listen to My voice; I know them, and they follow Me. I give them eternal life, and they will never perish. No one can snatch them away from Me." John 10:27-28

Your own ears will hear Him. Right behind you a voice will say, "This is the way you should go," whether to the right or to the left. Isaiah 30: 21

Mortals make elaborate plans, but God has the last word. Put God in charge of your work, then what you've planned will take place. We plan the way we want to live, but only God makes us able to live it. Proverbs 16:1, 3, 9 MSG

Since we are living by the Spirit, let us follow the Spirit's leading in every part of our lives. Galatians 5:25

"For I know the plans I have for you," says the LORD. "They are plans for good and not for disaster, to give you a future and a hope. In those days when you pray, I will listen. If you look for me wholeheartedly, you will find me. I will be found by you," says the LORD. Jeremiah 29:11-14A

Show me the right path, O LORD; point out the road for me to follow. Lead me by Your truth and teach me, for You are the God who saves me. All day long I put my hope in You. Psalm 25:4-5

Talking to God

Oh, Lord, my God, there are times when I wish You would answer my prayers on a billboard or a sky-writer so I would know for sure what You want me to do with my life! It doesn't always seem obvious to me. So what am I supposed to do? Over and over, I have heard that You want me to read Your words and listen to Your voice, and to put my trust in You. I guess that doesn't happen immediately, does it, dear Jesus? I suppose it takes time to read, listen, trust and grow in faith. There -- I have answered my own question.

Jesus, what I do need to pray for is for time alone with YOU. Help me to make a firm commitment to spend time reading Your words and listening to Your responses, trusting in You and being obedient to what You tell me. Faith is not seeing, yet believing, so I may have to go out of my comfort zone or out on a limb. But I do know You will be holding up the branch!

Take away my fears and fill me with the Power of God, Himself! Give me courage and give me an obedient heart to follow Your lead in my life. After all, who could be better than YOU, the Almighty God, to guide me, lead me, and counsel me! I bow before your leadership in my life. Bless me, Jesus. Bless me to be all that You have planned for me to be. In love and trust, I pray. Amen

---

Let the morning bring me word of Your unfailing love, for I have put my trust in You. Show me the way I should go, for to You I entrust my life.
Psalm 143:8 NIV

58

Heaven

I feel very happy over the thought of an eternal life with Jesus! But what is Heaven going to be like?

[Jesus said] There are many rooms in my Father's house. I wouldn't tell you this, unless it was true. I am going there to prepare a place for each of you. After I have done this, I will come back and take you with Me. Then we will be together. John 14:2-3 CEV

But we are citizens of Heaven, where the Lord Jesus Christ lives. He will take our weak mortal bodies and change them into glorious bodies like His own, using the same power with which He will bring everything under His control. Phil. 3: 20A and 21

God Himself will be with them. He will wipe every tear from their eyes, and there will be no more death or sorrow or crying or pain. All these things are gone forever." Revelation 21:4

But let me (the Apostle Paul) tell you something wonderful, a mystery I'll probably never fully understand. We're not all going to die -- *but* we are all going to be changed. You hear a blast to end all blasts from a trumpet, and in the time that you look up and blink your eyes -- it's over. On signal from that trumpet from Heaven, the dead will be up and out of their graves, beyond the reach of death, never to die again. At the same moment and in the same way, we'll all be changed. In the resurrection scheme of things, this has to happen: everything perishable taken off the shelves and replaced by the imperishable, this mortal replaced by the immortal. 1 Corinthians 15:51-53 MSG

But if you remain faithful even when facing death, I will give you the crown of life. Revelation 2:10B

Talking to God

What joy I have, oh, precious Jesus, knowing I am Your child, and You are preparing a place for me in Your Heavenly home! I know for certain that my inheritance is secure -- a glorious body, a magnificent dwelling, a new heaven, and a new earth. But the best of all is YOU, Father, Jesus, and Your Holy Spirit! You will be worshiped and glorified forever, and I will get to live eternally in Your Glorious Presence. Joy! Love! Peace!

Thank you for giving believers in Jesus Christ the extraordinary gift of heaven, and yes, it is a real place. Because every human dies, I need Your help to understand that hell awaits those who reject Your plan of salvation, and yes, hell is also a real place. It will be eternal anguish and eternal separation from love, for God is Love. It will be eternal darkness, for Jesus is the Light of the world.

Oh, that all of us would have a passion for the unsaved! Keep this in my memory Lord -- For You say to us, "At just the right time, I heard you. On the day of salvation, I helped you." Indeed, the "right time" is now. Today is the day of salvation. (2 Cor.6:2) Today is the day I need to share the good news of Jesus and the gift of Grace, salvation, redemption, and reconciliation. Today is really the only day I can share. Yesterday is gone and tomorrow may never come. Use me today, Savior Jesus, as I pray in Your name. Amen

---

Those who believe in the
LORD
never see each other for the last time.
Old German Proverb

Peace

I am disgusted with myself. I have no peace in my life because I am always striving for bigger, better, more! I worry and stress over my messed up life.

Why is everyone hungry for *more?* "More, more," they say. "More, more." I have God's more-than enough. More joy in one ordinary day than they get in all their shopping sprees. At day's end I'm ready for sound sleep, for you, God, have put my life back together. Psalm 4:6-8 MSG

[Jesus said] "Peace I leave with you; My peace I give you. I do not give to you as the world gives. Do not let your hearts be troubled and do not be afraid" John 14:27 NIV

I prayed to the LORD, and He answered me. He freed me from all my fears. Those who look to Him for help will be radiant with joy; no shadow of shame will darken their faces. In my exasperation I prayed, and the LORD listened. He saved me from all my troubles. Psalm 34:4-6

Don't worry about anything; instead, pray about everything. Tell God what you need, and thank Him for all He has done. Then you will experience God's peace, which exceeds anything we can understand. His peace will guard your heart and minds as you live in Christ Jesus. Philippians 4:6-7

The one who blesses others is abundantly blessed; those who help others are helped. Proverbs 11:25 MSG

Those who are controlled by the Holy Spirit think about things that please the Spirit. Letting the Spirit control your mind leads to life and peace. Romans 8:5B and 6B

Talking to God

Oh, Lord, my God, I have just read that a mind controlled by the Spirit will give me life and peace. I know for sure that my mind is NOT controlled by the Spirit. Would you please help me, God? I really do want to change. Lead me to Bible verses that will speak to me about peace. Help me to spend time alone with you, reading my Bible. I do have one, you know, but I haven't read it very much. Give me strength to read every day, even for 15 minutes.

I guess that if I am disgusted with my striving for more, overspending, and worrying about my credit cards, I need to change the way I live -- a real lifestyle change. I know You can help me, Jesus. Just look at what You did with the disciples. What a ragtag team of uneducated fishermen, tax collectors, even doubters. The Holy Spirit really changed them into confident, powerful preachers and teachers, and missionaries! Change me, too!

I also just read that I need to pray more and thank you God for everything -- even the mess of my life. I do thank you for this little book which has led me to an awareness of how I live; an awareness of how selfish I have been. Having the latest phone is more important to me than making sure children have food to eat. Please change me, Lord, and I am trusting that You will! Praise God for second chances. I intend to search for peace in my life and find it! With Your help, dear Jesus, I will. Amen

Write down your Bible-reading time schedule.

Write down negative habits you will change in your life. Pray over them. "I can do all things through Christ who strengthens me." Philippians 4:13

Giving Back to God

I am sad about my selfishness. If I go to church, I may throw a buck or two into the offering. Yet I think nothing of spending $100 at a restaurant or shopping mall. I am ashamed of myself.

For the love of money is the root of all kinds of evil. And some people, craving money, have wandered from the true faith and pierced themselves with many sorrows.   1 Timothy 6:10

You should remember the words of the Lord Jesus: "It is more blessed to give than to receive."   Acts 20:35B

[Jesus said] "Give, and you will receive. Your gift will return to you in full -- pressed down, shaken together to make room for more, running over, and poured into your lap. The amount you give will determine the amount you get back."   Luke 6:38

Bring the whole tithe into the storehouse, that there may be food in My house. Test Me in this," says the LORD Almighty, "and see if I will not throw open the floodgates of heaven and pour out so much blessing that there will not be room enough to store it." Malachi 3:10   NIV

[Jesus said] "Yes, a person is a fool to store up earthly wealth but not have a rich relationship with God."   Luke 12:21

Even if we feel guilty, God is greater than our feelings, and He knows everything.   1 John 3:20

For a greedy person is an idolater, worshiping the things of this world. Ephesians 5:5B

Talking to God

Gracious Lord, You are the God of generosity and the God of all good. Your complete mercy falls on us every morning. "When You open Your hand, You satisfy the hunger and thirst of every living thing." (Psalm 145:16) And when You give, it is not in a stingy way, but with the fullness of Your generous love. Help me to appreciate Your overflowing abundance in my life. I deserve nothing, yet You give me everything.

I pray for wisdom in dealing with my finances, and in fact, I know You will give me wisdom when I ask for it. It says in Scripture, "If you need wisdom, ask our generous God, and He will give it to you. He will not rebuke you for asking. But when you ask Him, be sure that your faith is in God alone." (James 1:5-6) I am now praying for my faith, as well as for wisdom. My faith and trust can never be in money. I know that, but sometimes I do not live like that! I have a double standard, and I ask for complete forgiveness.

Give me a heart to see people in need. Give me an awareness of how I can give back to You generously. Teach me to tithe, and better yet, teach me to worship You with my tithes and offerings. For all I have is a gift from You. Everything in the entire world belongs to You. On top of earthly blessings of money, job, food, clothing, YOU give the eternal gift of righteousness through our Savior, Jesus, who is also our Lord and Master. Today I bow before You and nail my selfishness to the cross where I find complete forgiveness. Thank You, as I pray in His name. Amen

---

God doesn't look at just what we give.
He also looks at what we keep.
Randy Alcorn
The Treasure Principle

The Church of Jesus Christ

What is it? I am confused. Is it just a building? Is it a denomination that goes into the building? What is meant by the church of Jesus Christ? If I believe in Him, am I in the church?

All this energy issues from Christ: God raised Him from death and set Him on a throne in deep heaven, in charge of running the universe, everything from galaxies to governments, no name and no power exempt from His rule. And not just for the time being, but *forever*. He is in charge of it all, has the final word on everything. At the center of all this, Christ rules the church. The church, you see, is not peripheral to the world; the world is peripheral to the church. The church is Christ's body, in which He speaks and acts, by which He fills everything with His Presence. Ephesians 1:20-23 MSG

(Apostle Paul said) "So guard yourselves and God's people. Feed and shepherd God's flock -- His church, purchased with His own blood".... Acts 20:28A

And you are living stones that God is building into His spiritual temple. What's more, you are His holy priests. 1 Peter 2:5A

The human body has many parts, but the many parts make up one whole body. So it is with the body of Christ. Some of us are Jews, some are Gentiles, some are slaves, and some are free. But we have all been baptized into one body by one Spirit, and we all share the same Spirit.......All of you together are Christ's body, and each of you is a part of it. 1 Corinthians 12:12-13 and 27

The churches became stronger in their faith, and each day more people put their faith in the Lord. Acts 16:5 CEV

Talking to God

Oh, Jesus, Lord of the church, thank you for desiring all people to be a part of Your church, that body of believers all over the world, who have faith in Jesus Christ and have been filled with the Holy Spirit. Yes, even insignificant me has the Holy Spirit inside my heart and mind. What a joy to have it, and to know that I have it! Your Spirit Power keeps me growing in my faith, making it stronger, wider, deeper, always looking for new ways to serve You by serving others.

Your church is worldwide, and I belong to a family of brothers and sisters in Christ all over the world. I do know that Your Word will not return to You void, and the gates of hell will not prevail against Your church. There is always victory in Jesus!

Your church is also local, the body of believers in one place. Bless both the worldwide church and the local churches with the Word, Godly worship, outreach to others, and the fervent love of Christ. Help each person to commit themselves to faithful worship of the King of Kings and Lord of Lords. Bless each individual to be devoted to each other as Scripture says the first believers were. Keep us strong, never lukewarm, in Jesus. Amen

---

One hundred religious persons knit into a unity by careful organization do not constitute a church any more than eleven dead men make a football team.

A. W. Tozer

Getting Old

I am fearful about getting old. There are so many unknowns -- will I be alone? Will I be healthy? Will I have the proper resources to live? Help!

I have cared for you since you were born. Yes, I carried you before you were born. I will be your God throughout your lifetime -- until you hair is white with age. I made you, and I will care for you. I will carry you along and save you. Isaiah 46:3B-4

Once I was young, and now I am old. Yet I have never seen the godly abandoned or their children begging for bread. The godly always give generous loans to others, and their children are a blessing. Psalm 37:25-26

But the godly will flourish like palm trees and grow strong like the cedars of Lebanon. For they are transplanted to the LORD's own house. They flourish in the courts of our God. Even in old age they will still produce fruit; they will remain vital and green. They will declare, "The LORD is just! He is my rock! There is no evil in Him!" Psalm 92:12-15

Don't be misled -- you cannot mock the justice of God. You will always harvest what you plant. Those who live only to satisfy their own sinful nature will harvest decay and death from that sinful nature. But those who live to please the Spirit will harvest everlasting life from the Spirit. So let's not get tired of doing what is good. At just the right time we will reap a harvest of blessing if we don't give up. Galatians 6:7-9

For we know that when this earthly tent we live in is taken down (that is, when we die and leave this earthly body), we will have a house in heaven, an eternal body made for us by God Himself and not by human hands. 2 Corinthians 5:1

Talking to God

God of my entire being, I thank you for the lifetime of blessings You have showered upon me. Not just for the major blessings of family and friends, but for all the daily, consistent blessings that Your Hand provides. You have been generous to me! When I was young and my faith was little, You, O Holy God, grew me spiritually through Your words and Spirit. Thank You.

When troubles and heart-breaking seasons came into my life, my faith was tested, and I failed. But You never failed! Even though I asked You to leave me alone, and I deserted You, You never deserted me. Your faithfulness was a steady, daily gift, even when I did not understand, even when I rebelled, even if I was angry with You. "The faithful love of the LORD never ends! His mercies never cease. Great is His faithfulness; His mercies begin afresh each morning." (Lamentations 3:22-23) That Bible verse is absolute truth, for it describes Your love and patience with me. It describes YOU, Papa. Every morning Your mercy and grace are there when my eyes open for the new day. Each day is a fresh start with You, Lord.

And now....as I enter the last season of my life, let my steadfast love and faith in You be "Oh, that You would bless me and expand my territory!" (1 Chronicles 4:9) Just as Jabez prayed, so I pray. Stretch me in my faith. Use me to do ALL the good deeds you planned for me long ago...I want to do them Papa. I don't want to miss out on one thing You have planned for me! Then, You can take me Home. I pray with expectation. Amen

As you age, what new fears has Satan lied to you about? Write them here and pray for the Holy Spirit to give you peace.

Ask God to show you good deeds He has planned for you to do.

Forgiveness

There are people who have hurt me so terribly I have trouble forgiving them. Some of my painful feelings go back a long time. I want to let go.

Stop being bitter and angry and mad at others. Don't yell at one another or curse each other or ever be rude. Instead, be kind and merciful, and forgive others, just as God forgave you because of Christ. Ephesians 4:31-32 CEV

For His Spirit joins with our spirit to affirm that we are God's children. And since we are His children, we are His heirs. In fact, together with Christ we are heirs of God's glory. But if we are to share His glory, we must also share His suffering. Rom. 8:16-17

Then Peter came to [Jesus] and asked, "Lord, how often should I forgive someone who sins against me? Seven times?" "No, not seven times," Jesus replied, "but seventy times seven!" Matthew 18:21-22

[Jesus said] "...and forgive us our sins, as we have forgiven those who sin against us." Matthew 6:12

But Joseph replied [to his brothers] "Don't be afraid of me. Am I God, that I can punish you? You intended to harm me, but God intended it all for good." Genesis 50:19-20A

Commit everything you do to the LORD. Trust Him, and He will help you. He will make your innocence radiate like the dawn, and the justice of your cause will shine like the noonday sun. Psalm 37:5-6

And we know that God causes everything to work together for the good of those who love God and are called according to His purpose for them. Romans 8:28

Talking to God

Dear Jesus, my heart aches and my mind never completely forgets the hurts of my past. You know all about it, Papa, because You know everything about me. You know how stubborn I can be regarding forgiveness. You know how I can hang on to mistakes other people have made, without recognizing my own mistakes! Sometimes I slip into self-pity, Lord, and that is so wrong, because it becomes a quick trip to bitterness and a heart of stone. Dear Jesus, I do not want a heart of stone.

You have told me that "despite all these things, overwhelming victory is ours through Christ, who loved us." (Romans 8:37) I can have victory in Jesus! But I choose self-pity. I choose hatred. I choose to hang on to my miserable feelings. It's debilitating, dear Lord. I need cleansing. I need to be washed "by the blood of the Lamb." I need to forgive the hurts of my past and let go of the bondage that accompanies it. With forgiveness comes freedom, and I desire freedom, dear Jesus.

Help me through Your strength to forgive others as You have forgiven me. "Forgive us our trespasses, as we forgive those who trespass against us." That is my sincere prayer to You, the God of my salvation. Free me from the tyranny of not letting go, not yielding my hurt and pain to the light of Your forgiveness. Allow me to forgive ALL who have caused me pain, all who have hurt me, all who have not loved me as I think they should have. Then I will have peace in my life--Your peace. I will be out of the darkness into Your marvelous Light. I pray in the name of Jesus, who is Light itself. Amen

> God, I am a child of light. Show me old parts of my life where I still need to flip on the switch of the truths You are showing me.
> Bruce Wilkinson
> *The Prayer of Jabez Devotional*

How Do I Please God?

We hear a lot of "Thou shalt nots." What does God want us to do? I feel doubtful if I know for sure.

We ask God to give you complete knowledge of His will and to give you spiritual wisdom and understanding. Then the way you live will always honor and please the Lord, and your lives will produce every kind of good fruit. All the while, you will grow as you learn to know God better and better. Colossians 1:9B-10

But the Holy Spirit produces this kind of fruit in our lives: love, joy, peace, patience, kindness, goodness, faithfulness, gentleness, and self-control. There is no law against these things! Gal. 5:22-23

Jesus replied, "You must love the LORD your God with all your heart, all your soul, and all your mind. This is the first and greatest commandment. A second is equally important: Love your neighbor as yourself.".......... Matthew 22:37-39

Remember, it is sin to know what you ought to do and then not do it. James 4:17

See that no one pays back evil for evil, but always try to do good to each other and to all people. Always be joyful. Never stop praying. Be thankful in all circumstances, for this is God's will for you who belong to Christ Jesus. 1 Thessalonians 5:15-18

Do your best to improve your faith by adding goodness, understanding, self-control, patience, devotion to God, concern for others, and love. 2 Peter 1:5-7 CEV

Three times I begged the Lord to make this suffering go away. But He replied, "My gift of undeserved grace is all you need. My power is strongest when you are weak." 2 Corinthians 12:8-9A CEV

Talking to God

This is the first time I have prayed this kind of prayer. Father God, help me to be weak, not in my faith, but weak in accomplishments of self. Sometimes I think too highly of myself and my capabilities. After all, isn't it true that we are a country of self-made, successful people, pulling ourselves up by our own bootstraps!

And YOU say "My power is strongest when I am weak." If that is true, and it is, then my desire is to be weak.

In weakness, Your Holy Spirit power will work in me to accomplish all that You desire, not me. Then I will become the person You desire me to be, not the one I thought I needed to be. Then You, Father God, will give me knowledge of Your will, and I will live to honor and please You.

I ask the Holy Spirit to produce in me the fruit of love, joy, peace, patience, kindness, goodness, faithfulness, gentleness, and self-control. Wow! THAT would make me a "new person in Christ!" I know I will never attain perfection here on earth, but it sure is fun to think about it! Help me to become more like Jesus.

I bow before you, O Gracious God, and ask for Your blessings of growth in my faith. Then I will always be joyful. I will never stop praying, and I will be thankful in all circumstances, for I know that joy, prayer and thanksgiving are Your will for me in Christ Jesus. Allow me each day to serve You through my faith in Jesus. Amen

---

As long as we take glory from one another, as long as we seek and love and jealously guard the glory of this life -- the honor and reputation that comes from men -- we do not seek and cannot receive the glory that comes from God. Pride renders faith impossible.

Andrew Murray

Scripture -- The Holy Bible

Is the Bible complete truth? Is it never-changing truth? Is it really written by God? I feel that I need to have the authority of God as a solid foundation for my faith.

Since childhood, you have known the Holy Scriptures that are able to make you wise enough to have faith in Christ Jesus and be saved. Everything in the Scriptures is God's Word. All of it is useful for teaching and helping people and for correcting them and showing them how to live. The Scriptures train God's servants to do all kinds of good deeds. 2 Timothy 3:15-17 CEV

Then [Jesus] opened their minds to understand the Scriptures. Luke 24:45

I have hidden Your word in my heart, that I might not sin against You. Psalm 119:11

Your word is a lamp to guide my feet and a light for my path. I've promised it once, and I'll promise it again: I will obey Your righteous regulations. Psalm 119:105-106

Put on all of God's armor so that you will be able to stand firm against all strategies of the devil......Put on salvation as your helmet, and take the sword of the Spirit, which is the word of God. Ephesians 6: 11 and 17

But Jesus told [Satan] "No! The Scriptures say, 'People do not live by bread alone, but by every word that comes from the mouth of God.'" Matthew 4:4

For the word of the LORD is right and true. Psalm 33:4A

Talking to God

Oh, God of the Universe, that I should have Your very words seems like a blessing too big to be true. But it is true! I have the words of eternal life, for I have the words of salvation in Jesus Christ. He is my Savior and my example for living a life in rhythm with God. Please, dear Jesus, open my mind to understand Scripture, just as you did with Your disciples.

Thank you for giving me this written testimony of Yourself. Of course, You had to give the condensed version -- for You are MORE than all the words, sentences, and books of the Bible. You are greater than my puny mind can fathom. How wonderful You are -- full of majesty and power. Your stunning Creation has been marred by sin. Just imagine what the New Heaven and the New Earth will be like. I can hardly wait!

Your words have endured for centuries, even though there have been countless cultures that have tried to bury or burn or belittle Your chosen Message to us, and that Message is Christ Himself, the good news of the Gospel. Your Word is Truth -- that is the reason for its stability in the midst of wars and tumult. You Yourself have stated "So is my word that goes out from My mouth: it will not return to Me empty, but will accomplish what I desire, and achieve the purpose for which I sent it." (Isaiah 55:11) So shall it be! May I, dear Lord, be faithful in my reading and memorization of Your commands and precepts. It is my desire to have Your word "hidden in my heart." In the name of my Savior I pray. Amen

> The Bible is alive, it speaks to me;
> It has feet, it runs after me;
> It has hands, it lays hold on me.
> Martin Luther

Discouragement

Some days I feel sad and discouraged. I try very hard to do the right thing and to do what others expect of me, but I get down. I get discouraged. It seems like no one is around to encourage me.

Do not be afraid or discouraged, for the LORD will personally go ahead of you. He will be with you; He will neither fail you nor abandon you. Deuteronomy 31:8

Be strong and courageous, and do the work. Don't be afraid or discouraged, for the LORD God, my God, is with you. He will not fail you or forsake you..... 1 Chronicles 28:20A

Don't be discouraged, for I am your God. I will strengthen you and help you. I will hold you up with My victorious right hand. Isaiah 41:10

As soon as I pray, you answer me; You encourage me by giving me strength. Psalm 138:3

No, despite all these things, overwhelming victory is ours through Christ, who loved us. Romans 8:37

Don't be afraid or ashamed and don't be discouraged. You won't be disappointed. Forget how sinful you were when you were young; stop feeling ashamed for being left a widow. The LORD All-Powerful, the Holy God of Israel, rules all the earth. He is your Creator and husband, and He will rescue you. Isaiah 54:4-5 CEV

Because of Christ and our faith in Him, we can now come boldly and confidently into God's Presence. Ephesians 3:12

Talking to God

Heavenly Father, I come to You now with praise on my lips and a song in my heart, for I know that You are my Friend and Encourager. Over and over again, You remind me that You will never leave my side, You will never forsake me or never stop loving me. I need those positive, encouraging words from You.

You say in the Psalms that You will never let the righteous fall, but occasionally I do stumble, and I am weak. I get discouraged by my lack of faith. Sometimes I seem to be on the mountaintop with You, dear Jesus, and then there are days when I am in the valley of despair, discouragement, or even self-pity. And some times, I even want to stay there. That is pathetic. Please forgive me. It makes me happy to know that my relationship with you, dear God, does not depend on my conduct or accomplishments. You know that I am made of dust. That's how weak I am.

Help me to be an encourager to the people around me, especially to my spouse, children, grandchildren, co-workers, and even my boss. Let me be generous with sincere compliments and words that will bring a smile, even to a stranger. In fact, smiling is really so easy, and it costs nothing. As a Christian and follower of the Lord Jesus Christ, I should always have a smile on my face!

Just let your love flow through me, sweet Jesus, and let my attitude towards others show how much I love You! In your name I pray this prayer. Encourage me to be an encourager. Amen.

Who in your family needs encouragement right now?

If you are discouraged, who will you go to for help?

Envy/Jealousy

I have a secret sin, and it is envy. I feel like I should have as much as my friends do in money, clothes, vacations, cars. I often get upset that I have less when I feel entitled to more!

Speaking to the people, [Jesus] went on, "Take care! Protect yourself against the least bit of greed. Life is not defined by what you have, even when you have a lot." Luke 12:15 MSG

Don't love money; be satisfied with what you have. For God has said, "I will never fail you. I will never abandon you." So we can say with confidence, "The LORD is my helper, so I will have no fear. What can mere people do to me?" Hebrews 13:5-6

For wherever there is jealousy and selfish ambition, there you will find disorder and evil of every kind. James 3:16

The LORD gave me what I had, and the LORD has taken it away. Praise the name of the LORD! Job1:21B

You want what isn't yours and will risk violence to get your hands on it. You wouldn't think of just asking God for it, would you? And why not? Because you know you'd be asking for what you have no right to. You're spoiled children, each wanting your own ways. James 4:2-3 MSG

Don't love the world's ways. Don't love the world's goods. Love of the world squeezes out love for the Father. Practically everything that goes on in the world -- wanting your own way, wanting everything for yourself, wanting to appear important -- has nothing to do with the Father. It just isolates you from Him.......but whoever does what God wants is set for eternity.
1 John 2:15-17 MSG

Talking to God

Oh, generous Father, You come to me with an open hand of blessing every day. I have more than I will every need, and yet there are times, I am sad to admit, that I want more or different or more fashionable or newer. Help me to be content with what You have provided for me. Help me to see all that I have instead of all that I want. Our culture places high priority on possessions, having the latest technology, new cars or trucks, bigger houses, and yes, one more pair of shoes.

Help me to be aware of the fact, that if I did not spend so much money on myself, I would be able to help feed hungry children in my neighborhood or sponsor a missionary. Awareness of my greed is the first step that I need. Help me, Holy Spirit. Secondly, teach me to "store my treasures in heaven, where moths and rust cannot destroy, and thieves do not break in and steal." (Matt. 6:20) If I give more of my income to You, Lord, I will be storing up treasure in Heaven! After all, You own everything in the world. So I am just giving back to You what is rightly Yours.

I know that You, God, love givers who are cheerful. You hate the evil of greed, envy, and jealousy. Your commandment says, "Thou shalt not covet." Give me a heart that is content to take second place, to give away more and keep less. I will reap what I sow, and I desire to sow generously. Give me Your power to accomplish this right now....there is no time like the present to begin! In the giving name of my Jesus, I pray. Amen

What "things' tempt you the most?

If you had more "free" money, what "treasures" would you spend it on?

Gossip/My Mouth

Gossip destroys people's reputations, yet I never hear any sermons on gossip. What some people post online is insensitive, even cruel, makes me furious when people hurt each other with words.

Those who control their tongue will have a long life; opening your mouth can ruin everything. Proverbs 13:3

Do everything without complaining and arguing, so that no one can criticize you. Philippians 2:14-15A

I said, "I will watch my ways and keep my tongue from sin; I will put a muzzle on my mouth while in the presence of the wicked." Psalm 39:1 NIV

And among all the parts of the body, the tongue is a flame of fire. It is a whole world of wickedness, corrupting your entire body. James 3:6A

So blessing and cursing come pouring out of the same mouth. Surely, my brothers and sisters, this is not right! James 3:10

A troublemaker plants seeds of strife; gossip separates the best of friends. Proverbs 16:28

Wrongdoers eagerly listen to gossip; liars pay close attention to slander. Proverbs 17:4

Without wood a fire goes out; without gossip a quarrel dies down. Proverbs 26:20 NIV

The soothing tongue is a tree of life, but a perverse tongue crushes the spirit. Proverbs 15:4 NIV

Talking to God

Oh Lord of my life, what is happening to our society, to our families and our friendships? No one seems to care about what they say or write online. Some people actually try to destroy each other through words, written and spoken. We need a wake-up call! Wake us up, Lord, to unkindness, blatant lies, even "little white lies". With You, there are no different kinds of lies; lies are lies, and you hate them!

Gossip spreads like wildfire, and truth is never desired. Help me to defend those who are not present to defend themselves. Help me to stop listening to conversations when I know they are nothing but damaging lies and half-truths. Make Christians aware of the need to be different in our online posts--give us words of kindness, encouragement, truth and clarity. Help me to have the courage to tell others to stop gossiping.

This falls under the spiritual fruit of self-control. The world we live in has no self-control, so please put it on the hearts of church leaders everywhere to remind us that truth is important to You, and You desire for us to have control over our mouths. Let it start with me, Lord, as I lift up this prayer in the name of the one who calls Himself Truth, Jesus Christ, my Lord. Amen

Which Bible verses are you planning to memorize?

How will you share your desire to stop complaining and gossiping?

Do you think OMG is taking God's name in vain?

A Letter from Paul, the Apostle Is Really a Letter from God.

To Fellow Believers in Christ,

This is my life work: helping people understand and respond to this Message. It came as a sheer gift to me, a real surprise, God handling all the details. When it came to presenting the Message to people who had no background in God's way, I was the least qualified of any of the available Christians. God saw to it that I was equipped, but you can be sure that it had nothing to do with my natural abilities.

And so here I am, preaching and writing about things that are way over my head, the inexhaustible riches and generosity of Christ. My task is to bring out in the open and make plain what God, who created all this in the first place, has been doing in secret and behind the scenes all along.

Through followers of Jesus like yourselves, gathered in churches, this extraordinary plan of God is becoming known and talked about even among the angels.

All this is proceeding along lines planned all along by God and then executed in Christ Jesus. When we trust in Him, we're free to say whatever needs to be said, bold to go wherever we need to go. So don't let my present trouble on your behalf get you down. Be proud!

My response is to get down on my knees before the Father, this magnificent Father who parcels out all heaven and earth. I ask Him to strengthen you by His Spirit--not a brute strength, but a glorious inner strength--that Christ will live in you as you open the door and invite Him in. And I ask Him that with both feet planted firmly on love, you'll be able to take in with all followers of Jesus, the extravagant dimensions of Christ's love. Reach out and experience the breadth! Test its length! Plumb the depths! Rise to the heights! Live full lives, full in the fullness of God.

God can do anything you know--far more than you could ever imagine or guess or request in your wildest dreams! He does it not by pushing us around, but by working within us, His Spirit deeply and gently within us.

In light of all this, here's what I want you to do. While I'm locked up here, a prisoner for the Master, I want you to get out there and walk--better yet, run--on the road God called you to travel. I don't want any of you sitting around on your hands. I don't want anyone strolling off, down some path that goes nowhere. And mark that you do this with humility and discipline -- not in fits and starts, but steadily, pouring yourselves out for each other in acts of love, alert at noticing differences and quick at mending fences.

You were all called to travel on the same road and in the same direction, so stay together, both outwardly and inwardly. You have one Master, one faith, one baptism, one God and Father of all, who rules over all, works through all, and is present in all. Everything you are and think and do is permeated with Oneness.

God wants us to grow up, to know the whole truth and tell it in love--like Christ, in everything. We take our lead from Christ, who is the source of everything we do. He keeps us in step with each other. His very breath and blood flow through us, nourishing us so that we will grow up healthy in God, robust in love.

Paul, the Apostle
(Written while imprisoned in Rome)

Selected passages from Ephesians Chapters 3 and 4
The Message, a Bible paraphrase written by Eugene Peterson.

Additional Prayers

Devote yourselves to prayer with an alert mind and a thankful heart. Colossians 4:2

For Change in My Life:

Father, I want to be a joy to You in new ways! I know that You are at work in me to break old patterns of thought and action. Break down the old barriers that I have in my mind. Please Father, may the Holy Spirit work in me, change my thinking, change my speaking, change my actions to do Your gracious will--to accomplish Your purposes and to fulfill Your plans for me.

Change me Father; change me Jesus; change me Holy Spirit for You live in me! Flush out all my fears, my anger, my frustrations and resentments, my guilt and failures. Flood me with Your love, Your power--the same power that raised Jesus from the dead.

Raise me up to be Your child, Your precious son/daughter dressed in my white robe, the robe You gave to me, washed white in the blood of Jesus Christ. Today, may I live to receive ALL You desire to give me--the fullness of God Himself. May I receive it ALL. In the name of my loving Savior, I pour out my heart to You. Amen

Elaine Kennelly

A Prayer for Power:

Dear Lord, I am forever dependent upon You, and sometimes I feel that I just can't do what You've given me to do. I feel overwhelmed and under-qualified. Please give me Your supply of supernatural power, that power which is made perfect in my weakness. Lord, I want a loyal heart, one that will be obedient when You call, one that will say "Yes" before You even ask. Send me Your Holy Spirit to equip me with all that is needed for the job. Pour Your strength and Your might into my feeble mind and body so that as Your purpose is fulfilled through me, YOU will get all the glory! I love you, Lord, with all my heart, and I desire to live in harmony with Your purpose for me. In Jesus name I pray. Amen

Written by Elaine Kennelly in
collaboration with a prayer by
Bruce Wilkinson
The Prayer of Jabez Devotional

A Prayer for Surrender:

Oh, Spirit of God continue to pray for me as You have promised to do. I most dearly desire a sweet spirit of surrender in my life. It has taken me so long to learn surrender, submitting ALL to You, my God and my Master. I still have not released every pain and every weakness. Show them to me and dredge them out of the deepest pits of my soul. Let my life be used, flaws and all, by Your plans for me. Wherever You put me, whatever work or ministry You give, help me to obey and trust in You! Allow me to live in the peace of Your Presence, praising and glorifying Your Holy Name. You are so worthy of praise! I love and thank You daily for Your precious love and generosity to me. In my Savior's loving name I pray. Amen

Elaine Kennelly

The Lord's Prayer:

Our Father, who art in Heaven. Hallowed be Thy Name. Thy Kingdom come. Thy will be done on earth, as it is in Heaven. Give us this day our daily bread, and forgive us our trespasses, as we forgive those who trespass against us. Lead us not into temptation, but deliver us from evil. For Thine is the Kingdom and the Power and the Glory forever and ever. Amen

Short Biblical Prayers

I love you, LORD; You are my strength. Psalm 18:1

"Be still, and know that I am God!" Psalm 46:10A

The LORD is my shepherd; I have all that I need. Psalm 23:1

"The LORD gave me what I had, and the LORD has taken it away. Praise the name of the LORD!" Job 1:21B

"I do believe, but help me overcome my unbelief!" Mark 9:24

I will sing to the LORD as long as I live. Psalm 104:33A

For I can do everything through Christ, who gives me strength. Philippians 4:13

Create in me a clean heart, O God. Renew a loyal spirit within me. Psalm 51:10

I went through fire and flood, but You brought *me* to a place of great abundance. Psalm 66:12B (Personalized by author.)

This is the day the LORD has made. We will rejoice and be glad in it. Psalm 118:24

You are my refuge and my shield; Your word is my source of hope. Psalm 119:114

Resist the devil, and he will flee from you. James 4:7B

I have hidden Your word in my heart, that I might not sin against You. Psalm 119:11

I will show you my faith by my good deeds. James 2:18B

We live by faith, not by sight. 2 Corinthians 5:7   NIV

Blessed are those who mourn, for they shall be comforted.
Matthew 5:4   NIV

...the joy of the LORD is *my* strength!   Nehemiah 8:10
(personalized by author)

LORD, hear my prayer! Listen to my plea!   Psalm 102:1

I say to myself, "The LORD is my inheritance; therefore, I will
hope in Him!"   Lamentations 3:24

Let us follow the Spirit's leading in every part of our lives.
Galatians 5:25B

"My grace is all you need. My power works best in weakness."
2 Corinthians 12:9A

Blessed are those who trust in the LORD and have made the
LORD their hope and confidence. Jeremiah 17:7

Restore to me the joy of Your salvation, and make me willing to
obey You. Psalm 51:12

Listen to my voice in the morning, LORD. Each morning I bring
my requests to you and wait expectantly. Psalm 5:3

O LORD, I will honor and praise Your name, for You are my
God. You do such wonderful things!   Isaiah 25:1A

Letting the Spirit control your mind leads to life and peace.
Romans 8:6B

F A Q'S

What are the foundational truths of Christian faith?

❖ The infallibility and inerrancy of God's Word, The Bible.

❖ The historic Creation of everything, as recorded in Genesis.

❖ The virgin birth of the Savior, Jesus Christ, the Messiah.

❖ Jesus is fully God and fully Man.

❖ The total depravity of all people. We are all dead in our sin.

❖ The substitutionary death of Christ . He died in my behalf.

❖ Christ's bodily resurrection from death.

❖ Jesus will return to judge the living and the dead.

❖ The resurrection of the dead. All people will be resurrected, some to heaven and some to hell.

Where are the 10 Commandments found in the Bible?
In the book of Exodus, chapter 20.

Is the "Golden Rule" in the Bible?
Yes, twice -- in Luke 6:31 and Matthew 7:12 -- "Do to others as you would have them do to you." NIV

What does the word "Amen" mean?
It is so! So be it! Used to express agreement.

What is the difference between mercy and grace?
❖ **Mercy** is compassion; an act of divine favor; withholding the punishment our sins deserve.
❖ **Grace** is God's free and unmerited gift of salvation through Jesus Christ.

How many books are in the Bible?
39 in the Old Testament. 27 in the New Testament. Total of 66.

What are the original languages of the Bible?
❖ The Old Testament was written in the Hebrew language.
❖ The New Testament was written in the Greek language.

What Bible translation is the best to use?
Most of the verses in this book are from the New Living Translation, which is a newer translation, but the NIV, which has been read for many years is also excellent. *The Message*----a paraphrase version, written by Eugene Peterson, has given us a fresh look at verses we have known for a long time. A Life Application Study Bible will give extra information on all verses.

What is an Epistle?
It is a letter. Many of the New Testament books after the first four Gospels of Matthew, Mark, Luke, and John are epistles or letters, most of them written by the Apostle Paul.

How many missionary journeys did Paul take?
Three. Some of his co-workers were Barnabas, Silas, and Mark.

Who wrote the book of Revelation?
The apostle, John, while exiled to the Greek island of Patmos.

About the Author

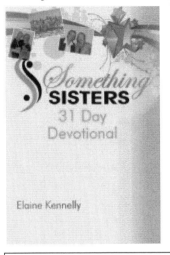

Elaine's first book is a tribute to friendship and faith for women over 50. **Something Sisters 31 Day Devotional,** is filled with devotions, prayers, and poems and can be easily personalized. It is written in conjunction with the website Elaine created SomethingSisters.com. This book is sold online at Amazon, Barnes and Noble, Books A Million, and other online sites.Also through the publisher, WestBow Press, A Division of Thomas Nelson, Inc.

There are seasons to life, and the most difficult season for me was the aftermath of our 18 year old son's death, and the fact that it was a suicide. My entire world collapsed, along with my neatly organized knowledge and understanding of God. I had known Him personally since I was a young child. I loved Him, read about Him, memorized Him, prayed to Him, studied Him, believed in Him, married in Him, taught school for Him, worshiped Him, and trusted Him. After years of life struggles with our son, I saw a rainbow, and thanked God, in advance, for healing Matt. He would have a testimony of overcoming! Two weeks later, Matthew took his life, and I had to ask myself, "What do I know about God?" The answer was -- not much. The collapse of my beliefs was quick and full of anger. Where was the God I knew? I had put my God in a little box, one that I could understand and even teach to others. I demanded answers from God, and when none came, I stubbornly stuffed all my feelings inside, and thought I could live life without Him. But God was faithful. He never left me. He healed me. He taught me, and through it all, I learned He loved me, more than I will ever know or ask or imagine. I learned about sovereignty, faith, forgiveness, and surrender. I learned to know God in all His fullness and to trust His unfailing, never-ending, faithful love for me. *Elaine*

Author Contact Information

Dear Readers,

I have a passion for getting the Word of God into the hands of people everywhere, and I love teaching how-to-learn more about God. It is important for us to see the supernatural power of God shine through the pages of His book, the Bible. Every time we read it, we learn something. Every time we believe it, we are changed. Remember, God tells us *"It is the same with My Word. I send it out, and it always produces fruit. It will accomplish all I want it to, and it will prosper everywhere I send it."* Isaiah 55:11

Feel free to email me at FaithOverFeelings@gmail.com I would love to hear from you. Ask your questions. Comment on your learning. Share your stories. What joy that would bring me! I will do my best to answer you personally.

This book is available for purchase at www.Amazon.com. Quantity pricing is available. Please inquire at the above email address.

I would also welcome inquiries regarding speaking to various groups, meetings, and retreats. I have led them in the past and would be honored to speak at your gathering in the future.

In the name of Jesus, who loves us and forgives us forever,
Elaine Kennelly

I pray that from His glorious, unlimited resources, He will empower you with inner strength through His Spirit.

Then Christ will make His home in your hearts as you trust in Him. Your roots will grow down into God's love and keep you strong.

And may you have the power to understand, as all God's people should, how wide, how long, how high, and how deep His love is.

Ephesians 3:16-18